THE LETTER AND THE SPIRIT

THE LETTER
AND THE SPIRIT

BY
R. M. GRANT

WIPF & STOCK · Eugene, Oregon

Wipf and Stock Publishers
199 W 8th Ave, Suite 3
Eugene, OR 97401

The Letter and the Spirit
By Grant, Robert M.
Copyright©1957 by
ISBN 13: 978-1-55635-958-3
Publication date 3/9/2009
Previously published by Macmillan, 1957

CONTENTS

CITATIONS AND ABBREVIATIONS

WE mention only those citations and abbreviations which might cause difficulty to the reader; they occur especially in Appendix II because of its lexicographical nature. There Cornutus, Heraclitus, and Porphyry are cited by page and line of the texts printed in the Teubner editions. The writings of Origen are cited, when available, in the Berlin Academy edition, *Die griechischen christlichen Schriftstellern der drei ersten Jahrhunderte*, by page and line except (at times) for the treatise *Contra Celsum*. Otherwise the citations are from the older edition of Lommatzsch. They are usually abbreviated *Princ.* for *De principiis*, *Ioh.* for *In Iohannem Commentarius*, and *C. Cels.* for *Contra Celsum*. Gnostic writers are cited sometimes by reference to the Church father who quotes them (e.g., Clement, *Str*[*omateis*], and *Exc*[*erpta ex*] *Theod* [*oto*]), sometimes by the numbers of the fragments collected by W. Völker, *Quellen zur Geschichte der christlichen Gnosis* (Tübingen, 1932).

SVF means H. v. Arnim, *Stoicorum veterum fragmenta*.

RE means *Realencyclopädie der classischen Altertumswissenschaft*.

PREFACE

In his tract *Of Prelatical Episcopacy*, John Milton denounces the Church fathers. "Whatsoever time or the heedless hand of blind chance hath drawn from of old to this present in her huge Dragnet, whether Fish or Sea-weed, Shells or Shrubbs, unpicked, unchosen, these are the Fathers." And Archdeacon Farrar, while finding this language too scornful, is ready to admit that "their glory is for the most part the glory, not of intellect, but of righteousness and faith".[1] Of Origen he says that "we can only come to the conclusion that the foundations of his exegetic system are built upon the sand".[2] More modern writers are often equally unenthusiastic, with the notable exceptions of Molland, Daniélou, and de Lubac.[3]

The present study is not a defence of Origen but an attempt to understand his methods in relation to the history of Greek allegorical exegesis and the related problem of the meaning of poetic and prophetic inspiration. It deals chiefly with his two principal early works, the treatise *On First Principles* and the *Commentary on John*, in the belief that while his views were modified in later works these two contain his principal contributions to the history of the allegorical method. In the course of the discussion an attempt will be made to depict the grammatical, rhetorical, philosophical, and theological grounds of his treatment of the Bible, and for the treatment of the Bible and other writings by other interpreters.

This study is not explicitly a theological treatise, but modern theological relevance will be found in the obvious analogies between ancient and modern literary criticism and theological problems. If nothing more, the study should show that the Fish and Sea-weed, Shells and Shrubbs, of antiquity are not altogether different from our own, and that we cannot blithely dismiss the intellect of the early fathers as contrasted with their righteousness and faith. Along the

---

[1] F. W. Farrar, *History of Interpretation* (London, 1886), 163–4.

[2] Ibid., 201.

[3] E. Molland, *The Conception of the Gospel in the Alexandrian Theology* (Oslo, 1938); J. Daniélou ,*Origène* (Paris, 1948); H. de Lubac, *Histoire et Esprit* (Paris, 1950).

way it may serve as a preparation for that future history of the allegorical method which, as Pohlenz has said, is *"dringend erwünscht"*.[1]

Our purpose is to trace Greek doctrines of poetic and oracular inspiration from the beginnings to the third century of our era, and to show some of the ways in which these doctrines were related to allegorical exegesis. Next we shall consider the development of belief in a primitive theology, obscured by poets, and to be recovered by removing interpolations, by allegorizing, or by a combination of the two methods. After this we shall turn to Hellenistic and other Jews and examine their methods of interpreting the Old Testament. Turning to Christianity, we shall discuss the theories of interpolation implicit in the exegesis of Jesus and, perhaps, in that of Paul. We shall find the second century marked by a series of conflicts over the interpretation of the Bible. In the third century the climax of allegorization is reached, partly in Clement, who reproduces Hellenistic Jewish exegesis, but more significantly in Origen. At the end we shall suggest certain parallels between ancient and modern developments.

I wish to thank those who have helped me in various ways. These benefactors include the John Simon Guggenheim Memorial Foundation; Professors A. S. Pease, A. D. Nock, and H. A. Wolfson of Harvard University; Professors J. H. Nichols, Ralph Marcus, and Daniel Jenkins of the University of Chicago; Professor J. H. Waszink of the University of Leiden; the Reverend Henry Chadwick of Queens' College, Cambridge; my father-in-law, Dean Douglas Horton of the Harvard Divinity School; and my father, Professor F. C. Grant of Union Theological Seminary, New York. In 1955 an earlier version of this book was awarded a prize by the Christian Literature Foundation.

R. M. GRANT

Federated Theological Faculty,
University of Chicago.

[1] M. Pohlenz, *Die Stoa* (Göttingen, 1948), II, 55.

viii

THE WISDOM OF THE ANCIENTS

As cultures grow old and complex, there emerges a longing for the simple greatness of earlier times. There comes to be a feeling that in more primitive times there was a closer relationship to nature or to the gods. The writers of an earlier day must have expressed the truth about life more adequately than more modern men. At the same time, there is an awareness that in some regards, at least, modern knowledge is more accurate, more in conformity with the nature of the universe, than that of the ancients. Out of this combination of nostalgia and philosophical awareness comes the notion that the ancient writers did not fully express what they meant to say about the world. They used enigmatic language which concealed their true meaning until the times were ripe for its fuller understanding. At times they said clearly what they meant, for some of their expressions are in agreement with modern ideas. At other times they simply employed conventional or obscure language which modern interpreters can and must reinterpret.

In part the mysteriousness of ancient poets can be explained as due to the quality of their poetic gift. For example, they may have been inspired by the Muses or by the gods, and their inspiration, perhaps brought about in a state of ecstasy, can have made some of their statements seem irrational. In such a case, modern interpreters can use rational methods to reduce their seeming irrationality to terms rationally understood. In part their mysteriousness may be due to the fact that as poets they intended to give pleasure to their audience. For this reason they would have used myths and metaphors, adorning a true tradition of pure philosophical or theological knowledge. Under these conditions, the modern interpreter will remove these myths and metaphors and thus penetrate directly to the truth.

It is obvious that both approaches to ancient wisdom or revelation are concerned with the perennial problem of faith and reason, and that both, while arising and flourishing in the context of Greek and Hellenistic philosophy, are much the same as those which have been found throughout Christian history and are still encountered to-day. While no historical parallel is exact, it is fairly plain that the method of those who stressed inspiration and sought to find a rational pattern in the utterances of poets is not unlike that of those to-day who try to find a biblical theology within the Old and New Testaments. And the method which found a true tradition apart from later accretions resembles on the one hand that of New Testament critics who have participated in the quest for the historical Jesus or, on the other, that of those who have wished to "demythologize" the biblical message.

In this chapter our primary concern, however, is not with modern parallels but with the ancient situation, in which the works of poets and seers were reinterpreted to meet the needs of changing theologies. We shall consider first the views of Greek writers before the Hellenistic age, and their teaching concerning the inspiration and interpretation of the ancient poets. Then we shall turn to the different situation which followed the rise of Greek preoccupation with oriental religions and philosophies, and examine the attempts which were made to correlate the learning of east and west. In both cases we shall be dealing with allegorical interpretation, but we shall attempt to investigate certain differences in emphasis which divide the later period from the earlier one.

HOMER, HESIOD, AND THE MUSES

Poetic Inspiration

The idea that divine inspiration is necessary for the creative work of the poet comes from the earliest days of Greek poetry. In both *Iliad* and *Odyssey* the aid of the Muses is invoked, and we find explicit statements that merely human powers are inadequate for the poet's task.[1] Though Homer doubtless appropriated a previously existing tradition when he invoked the Muses, it was he who set the pattern for later poets, especially the poets of the Hellenistic age. And whole belief in the Muses often becomes mere convention in later times,[2] Homer's invocations suggest the presence of genuine piety.

Hesiod similarly begins his *Theogony* by describing his dream-encounter with the Muses, who gave him a laurel wreath as a symbol

---

[1] Cf. O. Falter, *Der Dichter und sein Gott bei den Griechen und Römern* (Würzburg, 1934), 3–10.

[2] E.g., in Callimachus; cf. R. Pfeiffer, *Callimachus* (Oxford, 1949), 9–11; perhaps in Ennius, cf. J. H. Waszink in *Mnemosyne* IV, 3 (1950), 215–40.

of his inspiration. And they told him that they knew how to speak the truth (presumably the content of the *Theogony*) as well as falsehoods resembling the truth (doubtless the poems of other writers).[1]

Other poets continued to appeal to the Muses. Thus Pindar repeatedly refers to them as the authors of both the form and the content of his odes, and when the philosopher Empedocles uses verse to set forth his views on nature he appeals to the Muses for their aid. Knowledge of nature and of the gods comes from the gods. When Parmenides describes the eternal existence of the gods he is not content to invoke the Muses but allegorically journeys to heaven itself, where he learns the truth rather than the opinions of mortals.[2] Thus he may intimate that the source of his inspiration is higher than that of Hesiod.[3]

Not everyone, however, was convinced of the inspiration of the poets. The theologian Xenophanes, who held that the one God "ever abides in the selfsame place without moving; nor is it fitting for him to move hither and thither, changing his place", and that "in neither his form nor his thought is he like unto mortals",[4] not unnaturally made a direct attack on Homer and Hesiod because "they attributed everything disreputable to the gods".[5] There is obviously a "theology of the poets", but there is no reason to assume that it is true; indeed, philosophy shows that it is not true. And Xenophanes seems to be denying the inspiration of the poets when he says that "in the beginning the gods did not at all reveal all things clearly to mortals, but by searching men in the course of time find them out better".[6] He thus treats the poets simply as fallible, and indeed mistaken, men.

The Beginnings of Allegorization

His contemporary Pythagoras, who like him emigrated to south Italy, is said to have claimed that he descended to Hades, where he saw the souls of Homer and Hesiod in torment because of their false narratives about the gods.[7] His followers, however, soon came to regard the poets as true theologians, and interpreted their poems in

---

[1] Cf. K. Latte in *Antike und Abendland* 2 (1946), 152–63.
[2] Cf. C. M. Bowra, *Problems in Greek Poetry* (Oxford, 1953), 38–53.
[3] W. Jaeger, *The Theology of the Early Greek Philosophers* (Oxford, 1947), 93–4.
[4] Frag. 26. 23, Diels.   [5] Frag. 11.   [6] Frag. 18.
[7] Hieronymus of Rhodes in Diog. Laert. 8. 21.

harmony with Pythagorean doctrine.[1] And it is barely possible that the first allegorizer of Homer was related to the Pythagoreans. This allegorizer, Theagenes, lived at Rhegium in south Italy shortly after the coming of Pythagoras to nearby Croton.[2] Unfortunately the work of Theagenes is lost in obscurity. The allegories handed down under his name are actually those later used by Stoics, and we cannot be sure that any of them actually go back to the sixth century. All that is probable is that he tried to interpret the anthropomorphic gods of Homer as symbols of natural forces and of ethical and unethical behaviour.[3]

The next person to reinterpret Homer, Metrodorus of Lampsacus, wrote late in the fifth century and was clearly influenced by scientific philosophy and medicine.[4] He was a pupil of Anaxagoras, who had been exiled from Athens because of his insistence that the sun and moon were merely natural objects and because of his criticism of divination. Metrodorus evidently tried to adapt the traditional language of Homer to the new scientific insights. For him the Homeric gods were parts of the human body, while the human beings were the elements of nature. Thus Apollo was the bile, probably because Anaxagoras had said that bile caused acute diseases and in Homer Apollo brought about a pestilence. Demeter and Dionysus, essential to life, were the liver and the spleen. Zeus was probably the brain, Achilles was the sun, Hector the moon, while Agamemnon was ether, Helen earth, and Paris air.

This singular kind of allegorization met with little recognition. It survives only in fragments, and other followers of Anaxagoras identified Zeus with mind rather than the brain, Athena with art.[5] Metrodorus' thoroughgoing naturalism really made Homer religiously irrelevant. Perhaps it could be called a premature synthesis of science and religion.

Scientific Analysis of Inspiration

What was needed was an analysis of the inspiration of the poets. Without such an analysis there was no ground on which it could be

[1] P. Boyancé, *Le culte des Muses chez les philosophes grecs* (Paris, 1937), 121–4.
[2] Tatian, *Or.* 31, 120, Otto, "in the time of Cambyses".
[3] R. Laqueur in Pauly-Wissowa, *RE* VA, 1347.
[4] W. Nestle in *Philologus* 66 (1907), 503–10; Pauly-Wissowa, *RE* XV, 1476–7; *Vom Mythos zum Logos* (Stuttgart, 1942), 130–1.
[5] H. Diels, *Die Fragmente der Vorsokratiker* I (ed. 3, Berlin, 1913), 414.

claimed that the poet really possessed a true insight into the nature of the gods. The poetic appeal of the Muses was meaningless unless it too could be related to the new philosophies of nature. How did the poet know what he knew?

Already in the fifth century B.C. we find an attempt to analyse the nature of poetic inspiration in terms of the new philosophies of nature. The philosopher Democritus discussed this topic in his treatise *On Poetry*, and, while the treatise is lost, some of its leading ideas can be recovered from fragments in Cicero, Horace, and Clement of Alexandria. The names of these authors show us that his ideas were still influential in Graeco-Roman times. The first of them, Cicero (*Div.* 1. 80), tells us that both Democritus and Plato held that no poet can be great without some "madness" (manic or mantic inspiration). Horace (*A.P.* 295) parodies this view when he states that Democritus excluded sane poets from Helicon, the abode of the Muses. But Clement (*Str.* 6. 168. 2) quotes explicitly from Democritus: "Whatever things a poet writes with divine possession and a holy spirit are exceedingly beautiful."

Clearly Democritus believed that the poet's inspiration came from outside himself while his rational faculties were in a state of suspension, for example in sleep. In relation to the rest of his philosophy, this belief has been analysed by Delatte,[1] who has shown that the gods must have sent "images" consisting of very fine atoms to the poet through the openings in his body such as eyes and, especially, ears. But in his view the poet could not rely entirely upon the gods. In another work Democritus said that Homer acquired a divine talent (from inspiration) and created an edifice of varied poems (Dio Chrysostom, *Or.* 36. 1). This sentence implies that the poet's own art plays its part in the work of creation. Moreover, when Democritus said that Musaeus was the first to use the dactylic hexameter (Diels B 11), such use implies the presence of human creativity. There is no suggestion that the hexameter is due to the Muses or the gods.

Shorn of its atomism, the theory of Democritus recurs in the *Ion* of Plato. It is the god himself, says Plato, who speaks through Homer and makes proclamations to us through the poets (534 d). The poems,

---

[1] A. Delatte, *Les conceptions de l'enthousiasme chez les philosophes présocratiques* (Paris, 1934), 28–56.

then, are not human or the product of human writers; they are divine and the product of gods. The poets are nothing but interpreters of the gods (534 e).

The *Ion* is one of Plato's earliest works, and his whole doctrine on inspiration is not to be found in it. Over a period of time he came to value poetry less highly as compared with philosophy (he himself continues to invoke the Muses). In the very late *Laws* he criticized poets severely, and already in the *Phaedrus* (244 ff.) he set up an ascending scale of inspiration: that of the seer, that of the priest, that of the Muses (for both poets and statesmen), and that of the philosopher. Philosophy is a gift of the gods (*Tim.* 47 b). It is the highest gift because it is the most rational.

Since poetry is not so rational, even its greatest examples (as W. J. Verdenius has observed[1]) remain enigmatic, for the irrational origin of the poet's wisdom makes it impossible to call him to account about the meaning of his words. Therefore it seems wisest to abstain from definite exegesis. In this way Plato moves away from the doctrine in the *Ion*, and points toward his later distinction between the seer, who sees visions and utters words in a state of frenzy, and the prophet, who remains in his right mind and interprets these visions and voices (*Tim.* 71 e). We shall later see early Christians trying to make similar distinctions.

The process of rationalization which we observe in Plato also took place in the thought of his pupil Aristotle. The young Aristotle believed in the existence of prophetic powers which sleep within the soul; later he came to deny their existence and to treat dreams psychologically by using parallels from natural history. And when he discussed the inspiration of poetry in his *Poetics* he claimed that it was entirely due to natural causes.[2]

Stoic Allegorization

The Stoic teachers of the Hellenistic age combined the rationalism of Aristotle with a thoroughgoing allegorization of the poets. For the Stoics, God was not anthropomorphic; he (or rather, it) was the cosmic rational principle which produced and maintained the order of nature. Anthropomorphic descriptions of the gods therefore had to

---

[1] *Mimesis* (Leiden, 1949), 7.   [2] W. Jaeger, *Aristotle* (Oxford, 1934), 162.

have some meaning other than a literal one. Again, in their view a mysterious primitive tie bound the names of things to the things themselves. Names were "innate" rather than products of conventional usage. If one could understand a name (usually in terms of etymology) one could understand the thing of which it was the name. This semantic principle was combined with the theological doctrine to produce a philosophical reinterpretation of Homer and Hesiod.

Zeno, the founder of the school, stated that Homer wrote some things in accordance with opinion, presumably that of his contemporaries, and others in accordance with truth. Thus, says Dio Chrysostom, Zeno thought that he could avoid the notion that Homer contradicted himself.[1] The true statements were undoubtedly those which agreed with Stoic theology. The others included the names of the gods, which according to Zeno's etymologizing showed that they were elements or forces of nature. And he passed from Homer to Hesiod, interpreting the latter poet in such a way that, as Epicurean critics said, "he entirely removes the customary and traditional understandings of the gods" and makes their names refer to "mute and inanimate things".[2]

We possess a remark from Zeno's successor Cleanthes which shows the relation between poetry and philosophical understanding: "Though philosophical reason is able to make an adequate proclamation concerning divine and human matters, mere prose does not have expressions suited to the divine powers, and metres and tunes and rhythms especially reach the mark." [3] Therefore Cleanthes proceeded to try to "accommodate the sayings of poets to their system".[4] One of the most striking examples is his notion that Apollo is the sun because at various times the sun rises from various (*ap-allon*) places.[5] The other examples are no more convincing. But Cleanthes believed that he was discovering the true philosophical theology concealed behind the language of the poets.

The same situation is to be found in the work of his successor Chrysippus. God is one; but there are said to be gods and goddesses

---

[1] H. v. Arnim, *Stoicorum veterum fragmenta* (Leipzig, 1905–24) I, 274 (Dio Chrysostom, *Or.* 53. 4).

[2] *SVF* I, 167 (Cicero, *De natura deorum* 1. 36).

[3] *SVF* I, 486 (Philodemus, *De musica*, col. 28. 1).

[4] *SVF* I, 539.　　　　　[5] *SVF* I, 540.

because of the one God's active and passive functions.[1] In accord with this principle, Chrysippus wrote two books *On the gods*. The first contained philosophical theology. In the second he tried to accommodate (*accommodare* = *synoikeioun*) to this doctrine the myths of Orpheus, Musaeus, Homer, and Hesoid.[2]

In Cleanthes and Chrysippus we do not hear that some things are true while others are merely opinion. We hear that everything is to be accommodated. And, given the doctrine, perhaps of Chrysippus, that poetry "contains a reflection (*mimesis*) of divine and human matters",[3] we should expect this to be the case. Poetry as a whole has an allegorical significance.

Such an approach to ancient tradition was of course not confined to Stoics. During the fourth century B.C. some Pythagoreans had come to realize that the watchwords ascribed to Pythagoras had become meaningless. Some of the phrases consisted simply of scraps of archaic myth or archaic astronomy. To be told not to eat beans was not as impressive from the lips of a Pythagorean as it had been from Pythagoras himself. Therefore in order to make the watchwords meaningful a certain Androcydes produced a treatise *On Pythagorean Symbols*, in which he gave them a moral meaning in harmony with the developed teaching of the school. He interpreted them as "enigmas", dark sayings which required allegorization. In this form they were transmitted to the Hellenistic world, and to the Church father Clement of Alexandria, who used Androcydes to justify his own allegorizing work.[4]

Grammarians at Pergamum also joined the allegorizing movement. The most prominent of them, Crates of Mallos, regarded Homer as an astronomer and geographer. In the *Iliad* he found an enigmatic statement which hinted that the world is spherical. He also found a scientific-minded Zeus measuring the universe, in Homer's description of Hephaestus' fall from heaven.[5]

Of course this kind of exegesis was not unquestioned. Plato had already rejected Homeric mythology from the studies of the young

[1] *SVF* II, 1070.   [2] *SVF* II, 1077.   [3] Diog. Laert., 7. 60.
[4] A. Delatte, *Études sur la littérature pythagoricienne* (Paris, 1915), 285–8; P. Corssen in *Rheinisches Museum* 67 (1912), 240–63.
[5] C. Wachsmuth, *De Cratete Mallota* (Leipzig, 1860), 23–7; K. Reinhardt, *De theologia graeca* (Berlin, 1910), 59–80.

8

élite in his *Republic*, whether the stories "are supposed to have an allegorical meaning or not". He added that a young person cannot judge what is allegorical and what is literal—though as Tate has observed he does not say whether this meaning is actually in the myths or not.[1] Other critics denounced Stoic exegesis. On the one hand, the Stoics misunderstood the nature of poetry. It was intended to provide not instruction but pleasure. On this ground the geographer Eratosthenes denounced Homeric geography and the Epicureans denounced Stoic allegorization.[2] On the other hand, the Stoic theology was false. Apollodorus of Athens criticized the Stoics for reading their false philosophy into the poets.[3] The Epicureans observed that the old poets had never suspected the existence of Stoic theology.[4] And from another viewpoint the Academic sceptic Clitomachus denounced their allegorization as purely subjective and destructive of traditional religion. It amounted to a confession that religion was really false, since it removed the gods as gods.[5]

Theory in the First Century

In spite of all criticism, Stoic allegorization continued to flourish and in the first century of the Christian era we find its methods and results set forth in the *Homeric Questions* of a certain Heraclitus.

The book of Heraclitus begins with an admission that Platonic and Epicurean criticism of Homer's morality would be justified if one took Homer literally. Actually, however, the "divine" Homer, accused of slighting (*oligoria*) the gods, used the method of *allegoria*. Verses found in the *Iliad* prove this. "Not I shall ever fight with the heavenly gods; we are childish if we wish to contend with Zeus" (6. 129; 15. 104). These and other verses to be taken literally prove that Homer's accounts of the gods' conflicts have deeper meanings. Actually he is "the great hierophant of heaven and the gods" (p. 100).

Here Heraclitus uses religious language to convey his meaning, just as in his preface he says that "we who have been purified within the sacred precincts by lustral vessels must trace out the truth concealed under the form of poetry". This religious language had become

---

[1] *Rep.* 378 d; J. Tate in *Classical Quarterly* 23 (1929), 146.
[2] Strabo, c. 7; K. Müller in Pauly-Wissowa, *RE Suppl.* IV, 20.
[3] Reinhardt, op. cit., 117–18.
[4] Cicero, *De natura deorum* 1. 41 (*SVF* II, 1077).   [5] Ibid., 3. 62–4.

customary in dealing with allegorization. The rhetorician Demetrius (*Eloc.* 101) states that "the mysteries are revealed in an allegorical form in order to inspire such shuddering and awe as are associated with darkness and night; allegory too is not unlike darkness and night". But while Demetrius evidently distrusts allegory, Heraclitus delights in it.

The method to be employed in discerning the wisdom of Homer is allegorization, the understanding of his poems as allegory. Heraclitus defines allegory as "speaking one thing and signifying something other than what is said" (pp. 5–6). In order to prove that allegory exists in Homer, he gives examples from Archilochus, Alcaeus, and Anacreon, and then cites metaphorical language used in the *Iliad* (19. 222–4). At this point Homer seems to be talking about farming but he actually refers to war. This kind of analysis was derived from contemporary rhetoric, in which metaphor was defined as he defines allegory. Since allegory was often treated as a continuous metaphor, Heraclitus' definition could readily be accepted.

Much of the *Iliad* really reflects "physical theory".[1] Apollo is the sun, Hera is the air, Poseidon is water, Athena is earth, Hephaestus is fire, and Zeus is ether.[2] Athena is also perfect prudence, while Aphrodite is foolishness or imprudence, and Ares is strife, while Dionysus is wine.[3] There are thus some ethical allegories in the *Iliad* along with the physical ones, but in general the *Iliad* is concerned with the elemental powers of nature as compared with "the ethical *Odyssey*". All the wanderings of Odysseus are ethical symbols.[4]

How does Heraclitus know that these are allegories? He tells us that Homer was not only a poet but a philosophical poet. He therefore used allegorical language, just as "the obscure Heraclitus spoke theologically about nature by using symbols" and Empedocles "imitated Homeric allegory".[5] Presumably Heraclitus has some theory of the transition from primitive allegory to modern clarity, but he does not state what it is. Reinhardt notes the Stoic origin of many of his explanations,[6] but Tate reminds us that he was essentially a gram-

[1] Cf. Appendix II, s.v. *theoria*.
[2] *Quaest.* 6–16, pp. 9–25; 25, p. 39; 26, p. 40.
[3] Ibid., 28, p. 43; 31, p. 46; 35, pp. 51–2.
[4] Ibid., 70, p. 91. [5] Ibid., 24, p. 37.
[6] K. Reinhardt in Pauly-Wissowa, *RE* VIII, 508–9.

marian, not a philosopher; in Homer he was willing to find one, two, four, or five primal elements.[1]

In the first-century treatise *On the sublime*, later attributed to "Dionysius or Longinus", we find a fairly elaborate discussion of poetic inspiration. The author states that a poet must, of course, possess a natural faculty of expression, but to this two further factors, largely congenital, must be added. One is a grasp of solid ideas; the other is a strong and inspiring (*enthousiastikon*) emotion, coming as if diffused inspiringly (*enthousiastikōs*) by some madness and spirit.[2] From this inspiring emotion comes the "fantasy", the idea which enters the mind and results in speech. Under this influence the poet seems to see what he describes and to set it before the eyes of his audience,[3] and in many instances he is led to mythical exaggeration, far beyond what is credible.[4] This inspiration can be compared with that of the Pythian oracle at Delphi. The prophetess is impregnated by a "divine breath" and a "supernatural power" from the earth.[5]

The two factors, solid ideas and inspiring emotion, apparently produce conflicting results, for in some passages the poets use myths which on the surface are godless and immoral and must be taken allegorically;[6] other passages "represent the divine nature in its true attributes, pure, majestic, unique".[7] This true and sublime representation is exemplified in the opening words of the cosmogony written by the law-giver of the Jews.[8]

The two factors are united by the use of the allegorical method, for it reinterprets the surface godlessness and immorality in harmony with the truths clearly expressed by the poet. In other words, the ultimate criterion is not divine inspiration but knowledge of philosophical truth. And when the author calls this knowledge "largely congenital" we may wonder whether any real place is left for inspiration by a power outside the poet himself.[9]

We shall cite only one more example, from the end of the first century, to show what Greek writers thought about inspiration and interpretation. Dio Chrysostom has a very high doctrine of inspiration.

---

[1] J. Tate in *Classical Quarterly* 28 (1934), 109.
[2] *De subl.* 8. 1, 4.   [3] Ibid., 15. 1–2.   [4] Ibid., 15. 8.
[5] Ibid., 13. 2.   [6] Ibid., 9. 7.   [7] Ibid., 9. 8.   [8] Ibid., 9. 9.
[9] "Etwas Göttliches", W. Kroll, *Studien zum Verständnis der römischen Literatur* (Stuttgart, 1924), 33.

"The words of men and all their sophistical reasonings", he says, "are worth nothing compared with inspiration and report from the gods; for whatever wise and true words were ever humanly spoken concerning the gods and the universe came into the souls of men not without the divine will and intervention through the ancient prophetic and divine men."[1] Again, in discussing a city whose inhabitants "wish to hear nothing but Homer", he speaks of "the divine poets who learned from the Muses" and describes Homer and Hesiod as men "to whom there came a brief utterance from the Muses, a kind of inspiration of the divine nature and truth, like a flash of light shining from an unseen fire".[2] Yet at another point Dio can say that the "truest and most perfect exegete and prophet of the divine nature" is the philosopher,[3] thus following Plato rather than the poets. Dio was a rhetorician. That is to say that his idea of inspiration tended to vary in relation to his audience. But philosophical and poetic inspiration could be reconciled through the allegorical method, and Dio very often uses it. Truth is one, and it is primarily the truth as known in the Stoic system.[4]

Plutarch on Inspiration

We have now seen that in spite of some criticism there was widespread acceptance in antiquity of the notion that the poets were inspired by a power or powers outside themselves, that they spoke theological truth, and that this theological truth could be recovered by use of the allegorical method. The most complete discussion of inspiration and interpretation which we possess is given by the Delphic priest and *littérateur* Plutarch, writing at the end of the first century and the beginning of the second. In his works we find an attempt to provide a rational explanation of inspiration and of the ambiguity of oracular utterances.

The ultimate source of inspiration is analysed in two of Plutarch's works. In the *Amatorius* he declares that Plato was right in speaking

---

[1] *Or.* 1. 57; this passage and the following one were noted by E. Hatch, *The Influence of Greek Ideas and Usages upon the Christian Church* (London, 1890), 51.
[2] *Or.* 36. 9, 33–4. [3] *Or.* 12. 44, 47.
[4] Cf. W. Schmid in Pauly-Wissowa, *RE* V, 858–61. In a *tour de force* proving that the *Iliad* contains nothing but fiction he rejects the allegorical method (*Or.* 11. 17–18); but this is not his usual view.

of a kind of madness or experience of enthusiasm which is not con-genital (as in Pseudo-Longinus) but comes from outside; it resembles the experience of being filled with a spirit.[1] The fantasies of poets, because of the power with which they work, are like dreams of those who are awake.[2] They come from "participation and sharing in a more divine power".[3] In the treatise *On the Genius of Socrates* he gives the same explanation: "The mind of Socrates, pure and passionless, and intermingling itself but little with the body for necessary purposes, was fine and light of touch, and quickly changed under any impression. The impression we may conjecture to have been no voice, but the utterance of a spirit, which without vocal sound reached the perceiving mind by the revelation itself."[4] What happens in such inspiration is that "the air is sensitive to the touch of higher beings, and is so modi-fied as to convey to the mind of godlike and extraordinary men the thought of him who thought it".[5] In these two passages Plutarch concentrates on the divine origin of inspiration, but does not entirely neglect the physical processes in which it takes place.

In his Delphic treatises Plutarch tells us more about the form of the oracular utterances. Here his thought seems to develop. In the treatise *On the E at Delphi* it is assumed that the oracles come directly from the god. God is a master of dialectic; when he puts forth am-biguous oracles he is exalting and establishing dialectic as essential to the right understanding of himself.[6] In discussing *Why the Pythia does not now Give Oracles in Verse*, however, Plutarch presents a different theory. One of the persons in the conversation argues that since the verses are the god's, they themselves should provide the criterion for metre and diction.[7] This argument is not acceptable. The god did not compose the verses; he "only gives the initial impulse according to the capacity of each prophetess".[8] The realm of revela-tion is thus limited to this initial impulse, and the human factor in inspiration is fully recognized.

> The strain is not the god's but the woman's, and so with the voice and the phrasing and the metre; he only provides the fantasies, and puts light into her soul to illuminate the future, for that is what inspiration is.[9]

---

[1] *Amat.* 16. 758 d–e.   [2] Ibid., 759 b.   [3] Ibid., 758 e.
[4] *De gen. Socr.* 20. 588 d–e.   [5] Ibid., 589 c.   [6] *De E apud Delph.* 6. 386 e–f.
[7] *De Pyth. orac.* 5. 396 d.   [8] Ibid., 7. 397 b.   [9] Ibid., 397 c.

Plutarch then uses analogies to illustrate his distinction between the god and the prophetess. God is like a creative artist who uses materials to produce his work; the prophetess is the artist's medium.[1] Again, the god is like the sun, the prophetess like the moon which alters the sun's rays and by reflection mediates them to the earth.[2]

In this dialogue Plutarch mentions the exhalations from the ground at Delphi, and in the more "scientific" treatise *On the Cessation of the Oracles* he ascribes oracular inspiration either to demons or to the equally demonic natural exhalations. Three explanations are given of the way in which these exhalations work. The soul of the prophetess may have an innate power of divination, warmed by the spirit (an exhalation from the earth) and dried by it; or it may be made tense and keen by chilling and condensation; or its rarefied places may be filled up and compressed by the exhalation.[3]

These explanations are justified on philosophical grounds. The most ancient theologians and poets spoke only of the final and efficient causes of inspiration, while the "physicists" discussed material and formal causes. The two sets of causes need to be combined so that both God and matter are given their rightful place.[4]

The oracles, then, owe their form not to the god but to the prophetess. And of the Pythia several things can be said. First of all, most of the ancient oracles actually were in prose rather than in verse. Second, those oracles which were in verse corresponded to the ancient environment in which poetry was the ordinary mode of expression. In those days the god "awakened and welcomed poetic natures".[5] Furthermore, he wished to protect the prophetess from tyrants and therefore spoke ambiguously. And metrical responses could be more easily remembered than those given in prose.[6] These explanations do not seem altogether consistent, since in some of them the metrical form is ascribed to the god, in others to the prophetess.

In any event, times have now changed and men prefer clarity. Some persons still turn the oracles into verse, but this is not the work of the prophetess.[7] Since men distrust metaphors, enigmas, and ambiguities,

---

[1] *De Pyth. orac.* 21. 404 b-c.

[2] Ibid., 404 d; for Apollo as the sun, cf. *De E apud Delph.* 21. 393 d.

[3] *De def. orac.* 40-1, 432 c-433 a.

[4] *De def. orac.* 48. 436 d-e; cf. 47. 435 f.   [5] *De Pyth. orac.* 23. 405 e-406 d.

[6] Ibid., 26-7. 407 c-408 b.   [7] Ibid., 25. 407 b; cf. Strabo 9. 3. 5. c. 419.

the god does not provide any more oracles of this sort. There is less enthusiasm for poetry and there is a more stable social situation.[1] Enigmas, allegories, and metaphors are a thing of the past.[2] Nowadays truth is sifted out from myth in prose, and philosophy prefers to instruct rather than to astonish.[3]

Evidently for Plutarch the highest philosophical authority is modern philosophy. He does not need to search the writings of the ancients. There are contradictions in the theology of Homer, for example, which prove that it cannot be taken dogmatically.[4] The Delphic theology, however, does contain hidden meanings, for example in the epithets of Apollo.[5]

Since it is the philosophical content which is important, we are not surprised to find Plutarch attacking Stoic allegorization, not because it is allegorization but because it is Stoic. The Stoics "make the gods atmospheric phases, or powers of the waters or the fire, infused therein". They imprison the gods in matter, rather than (with Platonists) leaving them free, as charioteers or steersmen.[6]

We shall later see that Plutarch upheld the notion of an ancient oriental theology which could be correlated with Platonism. In the Delphic treatises he only touches on the theme, referring to the notion of demons between gods and men as derived from Zoroaster and the Magi, or from Thrace and Orpheus, or from Egypt or from Phrygia.[7] The oriental sources are not so important as the Greek theories of inspiration and interpretation.

In discussing *Why the Pythia does not now Give Oracles in Verse*, he merely mentions a troublesome point which deserves fuller discussion. This is the notion that the oracles were collected, revised, and interpolated by a certain Onomacritus.[8] He rejects the notion that such editing took place, presumably because had he admitted it, he would have had to disentangle the original tradition from later interpolations. His analysis or oracular inspiration would have become much more complicated.

Theories of Interpolation

Among educated people in the Hellenistic age it was common

[1] Ibid., 25. 407 b; 28. 408 b.   [2] Ibid., 30. 409 d.   [3] Ibid., 24. 406 e.
[4] De aud. poet. 4. 20 c–f.   [5] De E apud Delph. 2. 385 b–c.
[6] De def. orac. 29. 426 b; cf. Amat. 13. 757 b.   [7] Ibid., 10. 415 a.
[8] De Pyth. orac. 25. 407 b.

knowledge that the works of the most ancient theological poets were not preserved in precisely the form in which their authors had left them. As early as the fourth century, two local historians of Megara claimed that Pisistratus, the sixth-century tyrant of Athens, had made interpolations in the *Iliad*.[1] They may have been referring to the notion, later widespread, that he was responsible for producing an edition, or the first edition, of Homer.[2] Josephus clearly reflects some such notion when he tells us that "people say that Homer did not leave his poetry in written form, but that it was transmitted by memory and later compiled from his songs; this accounts for the many contradictions in it".[3]

Some such idea must lie behind the work of the textual critics of Alexandria, beginning with Zenodotus (*c.* 325–*c.* 260). This critic tried to remove interpolations (*diaskeuai*) from the text of Homer, relying on four principles of criticism. Interpolations, he claimed, could be detected (1) if they broke the continuity of the poem, (2) if they lacked poetic art or were unsuitable to the characters of gods and men, (3) if they contained errors about ancient events, (4) if they differed from the usual style of the poet.[4] Zenodotus relied chiefly on the first two principles, and especially the second, with its opening for theological subjectivity; his successors, Aristophanes and Aristarchus, used the third and fourth and preserved the traditional text of their time while indicating doubts about verses or longer passages by the use of critical signs. It is a question whether Aristarchus (*c.* 216– *c.* 144) ever appealed to manuscript evidence in correcting the work of Zenodotus. Did he simply use the arguments listed above? His notion that Homer was an Athenian may be based on recognition that Pisistratus had edited the text; on the other hand, it may be derived from awareness of the importance of Athens as a centre of Homeric transmission generally.[5]

Nineteenth- and early twentieth-century scepticism about the use of manuscript evidence by the Alexandrian critics, as well as about the editing of Homer in the sixth century, is in process of modification. Mazon, for example, insists that Aristarchus, at least, made use of

---

[1] Diog. Laert., 1. 57; Plutarch, *Perseus* 20. 2.
[2] Cf. A. Gudeman, *Grundriss zur Geschichte der klassischen Philologie* (Leipzig, 1907), 10–11.
[3] *Contra Apionem* 1. 12. [4] Cohn in Pauly-Wissowa, *RE* II, 868.
[5] Mülder in *RE* IX, 1050–1.

ancient manuscripts,[1] and while he doubts that Pisistratus was responsible for the first edition, he suggests that an Ionian copy of Homer did come from Asia to Athens in the middle of the sixth century.[2] Bolling argues that both Zenodotus and Aristarchus used collations of manuscripts.[3] And Page, while unwilling to state dogmatically that Aristophanes and Aristarchus used manuscripts to prove that the *Odyssey* ended at 23. 296, urges that they were certainly right in their claim;[4] and the standard text of Homer was created at Athens in the sixth century.[5]

Whether the Victorians or the moderns are right in their analysis of the editing and re-editing of Homer, it remains a fact that Graeco-Roman writers believed, presumably not without some grounds for their belief, that Homer had suffered interpolation as well as omission, and that it was possible for critics to recover something like the original text.

A singular example of criticism is provided by the Christian writer Julius Africanus, who discusses a valuable magical incantation of the imperial age which he believes ought to be included in the eleventh book of the *Odyssey*. He explains its omission in the traditional text as due either to Homer himself or to the circle of Pisistratus. Homer may have omitted the verses because of the dignity of his work; the Pisistratids may have deleted them as alien to the "march" (*stoichos*) of the poem. Africanus does not care which explanation is preferred, and records the verses as "a most valuable product of the epic art".[6] He assumes that the incantation is either pre-Homeric or Homeric.

The Pisistratids were regarded as having edited not only Homer but also the Orphic poems. This work, involving not only redaction but sometimes composition, was ascribed to Onomacritus.[7] Did the idea of redaction have any influence on doctrines of inspiration and interpretation? At this point, as Guthrie observes, "the credulity of the very

---

[1] P. Mazon, *Introduction à l'Iliade* (Paris, 1948), 17–18.   [2] Ibid., 275.
[3] G. M. Bolling, *The Athetized Lines of the Iliad* (Baltimore, 1944), 32–7.
[4] D. Page, *The Homeric Odyssey* (Oxford, 1955), 101–36.   [5] Ibid., 143–5.
[6] B. P. Grenfell and A. S. Hunt, *The Oxyrhynchus Papyri* III, no. 412; cf. E. Hefermehl in *Berliner Philologischer Wochenschrift* 26 (1906), 413–15; R. Wünsch in *Archiv für Religionswissenschaft* 12 (1909), 2–19. Cf. Appendix III.
[7] O. Kern, *Orphicorum fragmenta* (Berlin, 1922), Test. 182–95.

pious must be taken into account". Since in their view Onomacritus himself was inspired, "the certainty that what he added was in accordance with the spirit of prophecy and truth would induce a state of indifference in which the line of demarcation between original and reformed theology would soon become blurred".[1]

Only the grammarians, whom we shall presently discuss, found such distinctions important. Thus the Christian grammarians Tatian and Clement insisted on the significance of Onomacritus' editorial work.[2] We do not hear of Orphic enthusiasm for the notion.

THE ANCIENT THEOLOGICAL TRADITION

Interest in Oriental Theology

Thus far we have been considering the views of those who dealt with the inspiration of Greek poets and seers and the interpretation of their utterances. In the Hellenistic age and after, however, another constellation of factors had to be taken into account. Egyptian theology had already impressed Herodotus, but the expeditions of Alexander more deeply and widely stirred the imagination of the Greek world. Fresh emphasis was laid on the ancient wisdom of the orient.

In the *Timaeus* of Plato an Egyptian priest is described as pointing out to Solon the incredible antiquity of Egyptian culture,[3] and in the young Aristotle's treatise *On Philosophy* the "ancient philosophy" was traced back to the Magi, the Egyptians, the (Greek) theologians, the Orphics, Hesiod, and the seven wise men.[4] Both in the Old Academy of Plato and in the Peripatetic school there was great interest in oriental theology, and as Jaeger notes, Aristotle's disciple Eudemus of Rhodes was "the first man to write a history of theology".[5]

Was Eudemus an "orientalizer"? In other words, did he trace the origins of Greek theology back to the orient? Certainly he gave an account of the cosmogonies of Orpheus, the Magi, the Sidonians, and

---

[1] W. K. C. Guthrie, *Orpheus and Greek Religion* (ed. 2, London, 1952), 107–8.

[2] *Or.* 41, 158 Otto; *Str.* 1. 131. 1–3.

[3] *Tim.* 22–4; on the whole subject cf. T. Hopfner, *Orient und griechische Philosophie* (*Beihefte zum Alten Orient* 4, Leipzig, 1925).

[4] Frag. 3. 6–8 Walzer; W. Jaeger, *Aristotle* (Oxford, 1934), 128–9.

[5] *The Theology of the Early Greek Philosophers* (Oxford, 1947), 5.

THE WISDOM OF THE ANCIENTS

the Egyptians, for we find his discussion summarized in the *Dubitationes et solutiones* of the sixth-century Neoplatonist Damascius.[1] But, as Wehrli points out, Orpheus does not follow the oriental theologians; he precedes them.[2] In Eudemus' discussions of other sciences there is not much enthusiasm for oriental contributions. When he wrote on the history of astronomy he apparently confined his remarks to Greek discoveries.[3] And in his history of mathematics he claimed that while arithmetic began among the Phoenicians and geometry among the Egyptians, these sciences were merely practical until the Greeks developed them theoretically.[4] Eudemus, then, cannot be counted as an adherent of the theory that wisdom came from the orient, although he was certainly interested in oriental theologies.

Theories of Interpolation and Borrowing

Real impetus was given this theory by Hecataeus of Abdera, at the end of the fourth century. According to him the Egyptians were the most ancient of all peoples, and some of their theological doctrines were paralleled by Homer and Orpheus.[5] Indeed, Homer visited Egypt and was instructed by the priests there.[6] Egypt was also the source of Chaldaean astrology[7] and of the Eleusinian mysteries.[8]

In Hecataeus' view the Egyptian theology was not the same as the popular religion. Actually the Egyptian gods were either powers of nature or deified dead men. And it was this theology which Moses derived from Egypt. Both the good and the bad in Judaism came from the Egyptian theology. On the one hand, Moses instituted the worship of God without the use of images because of what he had learned; on the other, because he was an exile from Egypt, he set up a way of life which was inhospitable toward strangers.[9]

Even the traditional notion that legislation came from the gods was taken from the Egyptians by various peoples. Among the Arians this

---

[1] Cc. 123-5, I, 319-23 Ruelle; F. Wehrli, *Die Schule des Aristoteles* 8 (Basel, 1955), frag. 150.

[2] Op. cit., p. 122.   [3] Ibid., frag. 143-9.

[4] Ibid., frag. 133.

[5] F. Jacoby, *Die Fragmente der griechischen Historiker* III A (Leiden, 1940), F 25, pp. 22-4 (Diodorus Siculus 1. 10-12).

[6] Ibid., p. 24. 20-4 (Diod. Sic. 1. 12. 10).   [7] Ibid., p. 28. 29 (Diod. Sic. 1. 28. 1).

[8] Ibid., p. 28. 31 (Diod. Sic. 1. 29. 2-3).   [9] Ibid., F 6, p. 14. 17 (Diod. Sic. 40. 3. 4).

notion was taught by Zathraustes (Zoroaster), among the Getae by Zalmoxis, and of course among the Jews by Moses.[1] The Greeks too have a similar tradition, though with them it is embellished by "fictitious myths".[2] Here Hecataeus differentiates the oriental tradition in its primitive purity from the additions or interpolations made among the Greeks presumably by poets. Orpheus, for example, made up his myth about Hades partly by describing Egyptian burial customs and partly by introducing fictions.[3] Some of Homer's notions were in turn derived from Orpheus.[4]

In Hecataeus we see the first full presentation of the "oriental" theory which we shall encounter among many later writers. There was a primitive true theology, handed down among oriental peoples but misunderstood and corrupted among the Greeks, especially by the poets. We can suspect, though we cannot prove, that this doctrine was set forth in his lost treatise *On the Poetry of Homer and Hesiod*.[5] He contrasted the original piety of barbarian nations, especially the Egyptians but including the Hyperboreans as well,[6] with the imitations made by the Greeks.

An analogous doctrine of decline and fall was presented in the first century B.C. by the eclectic Stoic philosopher Posidonius, who believed that while the first men simply followed the guidance of nature, the rise of various vices made religious legislation necessary both among barbarians and among Greeks.[7] This legislation was derived from the gods and proclaimed by ancient lawgivers, including such men as Orpheus, Musaeus, Zamolxis, and Moses.[8] Moses, who had been an Egyptian priest, instituted a pure, imageless worship among the Jews. Unfortunately his tyrannical and superstitious successors corrupted Judaism by adding dietary regulations, circumcision, excision, and other practices.[9]

Here we have a theory which goes beyond that of Hecataeus.

---

[1] J. Bidez-F. Cumont, *Les mages hellénisés* (Paris, 1938) II, 30, frag. B 19 (Diod. Sic. 1. 94. 2).

[2] Jacoby, op. cit., F 25, p. 61. 25 (Diod. Sic. 1. 93. 3).

[3] Ibid., p. 60. 34 (Diod. Sic. 1. 92. 3).

[4] Ibid., p. 62. 8 (Diod. Sic. 1. 96. 4–6 a).   [5] Ibid., T 1, p. 11. 8.

[6] Ibid., F 12, p. 17. 11–12.   [7] Seneca, *Ep.* 90. 4–6.

[8] Jacoby, op. cit., II A (Berlin, 1926), F 87, pp. 264–7 (Strabo 16. 2. 37. 761–2).

[9] Cf. K. Reinhardt, *Poseidonios über Ursprung und Entartung* (Heidelberg, 1928), 6–34; M. Pohlenz, *Die Stoa* (Göttingen, 1948) I, 213.

Hecataeus found Moses himself responsible for both the good and the bad in Judaism. Posidonius ascribes the good to Moses but the bad to his successors. Both agree that Moses brought the good from Egypt.

A prominent figure in this "oriental" movement was the grammarian Alexander Polyhistor of Miletus, who wrote in the first century, after Posidonius. He repeats commonplaces about Greek borrowings from the orient. Thus in his treatise *On Pythagorean Symbols* he says that Pythagoras was a disciple of Zaratus (Zoroaster) the Assyrian, and adds that he also learned from Galatians and Brahmans.[1] Alexander also reflects the attempts of Hellenistic Jews to show that all other cultures and, indeed, religions were derived from their ancestors. He cites Artapanus as authority for the story that Abraham taught astrology to the king of Egypt.[2] Artapanus also wrote that Moses (whom the Greeks knew as Musaeus, the teacher of Orpheus) taught the Egyptians their philosophy and was called Hermes by the priests.[3] Alexander, one of his sources, or one of his copyists became rather confused in dealing with so much tradition, for Suidas says that he said that the law of the Hebrews was given them by a woman named Moso.[4] He contributes nothing to our understanding of theory, but simply reflects the common interest in oriental origins.

At this point we should also mention Diodorus Siculus, whose first book is our source for much of the theory of Hecataeus. Diodorus took it over without acknowledgement. His taking it over suggests that the theory was alive in his own time, at the end of the first century B.C.

Interpolation Theories of Cornutus and Plutarch

This doctrine of an ancient theological tradition is explicitly combined with the theory of exegesis in the *Epidrome* of the grammarian Cornutus, who wrote at Rome soon after the middle of the first century of our era.[5]

Cornutus is highly important for our study, because in his treatise the points which had been stated in Hecataeus' work are explicitly

---

[1] Jacoby, op. cit., III A, F 94, p. 118. 13.
[2] Ibid., F 19 (Eusebius, *Praep. ev.* 9. 18).   [3] Eusebius, *Praep. ev.* 9. 27. 3–6.
[4] Jacoby, op. cit., F 70, p. 107. 29.
[5] On him cf. A. D. Nock in Pauly-Wissowa, *RE Suppl.* V, 995–1005.

worked out. He believes in the existence of an ancient theology, based on the ancients' correct understanding of nature but handed down in mythical form, in symbols and enigmas.[1] This theology was transmitted among the Magi, the Phrygians, the Egyptians, the Celts, the Libyans, and other nations which probably include the Syrians and Phoenicians.[2] It is more ancient than either Homer, who alludes to ancient myth, or Hesiod, who added mythical items to it.[3] The *Theogony* of Hesiod was based on a reliable theological source, but the poet was responsible for mythical details.[4]

The task of the exegete is therefore to recover this ancient theology by "demythologizing". He must refer (*anagein*) the items which seem to have been handed down in mythical form concerning the gods to the elements of nature.[5] He must not confuse the myths or transfer the names from one to another or treat irrationally what the poets added. These additions were made to the traditional genealogies by persons who did not understand their hidden meaning but treated them as fictitious.[6] The exegete can follow the etymological method of the Stoics, but he should be more restrained than Cleanthes was and should avoid the mere cleverness of Chrysippus.[7]

Much the same theory is presented by Plutarch, whose views concerning Greek inspiration and interpretation we have already met. In his treatise *On Isis and Osiris* he interprets the true and ancient theology of the Egyptians.

He claims that there is nothing irrational or mythical in Egyptian rites, since they are really partly ethical and partly historical or "natural" (8). Solon, Thales, Plato, Eudoxus, Pythagoras, and Lycurgus borrowed from them; and Pythagoras imitated their symbolic and mysterious method of presentation, combining his (or their) doctrines with enigmas (10). In hearing the Egyptians' stories one must not suppose that anything happened as it is described, but must interpret the content "religiously and philosophically" (11). This means that one must remove the unsuitable and irrelevant elements (12), such as the dismemberment of Osiris or the beheading of Isis; these are myths and fictions added by poets and logographers, who

---

[1] *Epidr.* 35, p. 76, 4–5 Lang.   [2] Ibid., 17, p. 26; 6, p. 6; 28, p. 54.
[3] Ibid., 17, p. 26; p. 31, 12–18.   [4] Ibid., 17, p. 28.   [5] Ibid., 35, p. 75. 18.
[6] Ibid., 17, p. 26. 19.
[7] Ibid., 31, p. 64. 17; 20, p. 37. 16; cf. J. Tate in *Classical Quarterly* 23 (1929), 41–5.

like spiders spin them out of themselves (19). In conclusion, Plutarch
states that the very ancient opinion, which passed from theologians
and legislators to poets and philosophers, was expressed not only in
writings but also in rites by both barbarians and Greeks. This very
ancient doctrine is that there is a cosmic dualism (45); Plutarch illus-
trates it from Zoroaster among the Magi, and Mithras, the Chaldaeans,
and the Greeks: Heraclitus (speaking literally, for once), Empedocles,
Pythagoras, Anaxagoras, Aristotle, and Plato (46–8). The theology
of the Egyptians is accommodated (synoikeioun) especially to the
philosophy of Plato.[1]

In a passage to which Andresen draws attention,[2] we learn that the
Orphic hymns and the Egyptian and Phrygian writings (logoi) make
evident that there is an ancient doctrine of nature among both Greeks
and barbarians, a philosophy of nature (physikos logos) concealed in
myths, largely hidden in enigmas and allegories (hyponoiai). Its interpretation is provided by the things done symbolically in religious
rites.

From these passages it is evident that, at least from time to time,
Plutarch espoused the doctrine of an ancient Graeco-oriental theology
genuinely philosophical but obscured by the later addition of myths,
enigmas, and allegories.

Grammarians, Gnostics, and Platonists

Plutarch's younger contemporary, the grammarian Philo of Byblos,
was also concerned with primitive oriental theology. He claims to
have translated into Greek the ancient Phoenician mythology compiled
by a certain Sanchuniathon either before or during the Trojan war.[3]
The true mythology, which has reference to natural forces and to
human beings, was composed by Taautos, whom the Egyptians call
Thouth, the Alexandrians Thoth, and the Greeks Hermes.[4] This
mythology was then interpolated with allegories and myths by the
later Phoenician hierologues. [5] Other theologians followed Phoenician
doctrine but misunderstood it because of these allegories; Porphyry,
following Philo, mentions Pherecydes, Egyptians, Zoroaster, and

---

[1] C. Andresen, Logos und Nomos (Berlin, 1955), 256.
[2] Ibid., 257; Eusebius, Praep. ev. 3. 1; O. Kern, Orphicorum fragmenta (Berlin, 1922),
316 (frag. 300).
[3] Eusebius, Praep. ev. 1. 9. 21.   [4] Ibid., 22–4.   [5] Ibid., 26; cf. 10. 39.

Ostanes.[1] Philo himself says that the Greeks treated the account as tragedy and took pleasure in myths; Hesiod is an example of this use.[2] However, by research in temple archives Sanchuniathon was able to recover the true original account, ridding it of allegories. He restored it, but later priests again interpolated it with allegories.[3] Fortunately Philo of Byblos was able to find it again.

We are not concerned with the authenticity of Sanchuniathon's account, which has been discussed by Eissfeldt and Clemen;[4] our only interest is in the theory of a primitive oriental theology, a theory common in the Graeco-Roman world. One striking difference between Plutarch and Philo is obvious. Plutarch was a priest and enjoyed cordial relations with the Egyptian priests who explained the true meaning of their relation to him. Philo was a grammarian, a layman who was exposing priestly frauds. Grammarians were reliable. Thus the ultimate source of Phoenician mythology was Taautos, who invented writing, while Sanchuniathon was a "polymath".[5]

There are remarkable similarities between the true ancient theologies of Philo and Plutarch. In both writers there is the notion that the stories about the gods are to be referred to stories about heroes or to natural phenomena. In both there is the idea that poets added mythical details to the original true account. For both a process of demythologizing is essential, just as it was for Cornutus, and before him, for Hecataeus.[6]

It must be observed again that Philo is suspicious of priests, for when we later deal with the Christian heretic Marcion we shall find a similar kind of suspicion, and a similar attempt to remove interpolations (chapter 4). Here we point out only that Marcion was a layman, on bad terms with the presbyters of the Roman Church and probably with the bishop of Smyrna,[7] and that in his view the

---

[1] Eusebius, *Praep. ev.* 1. 10. 50-2; cf. Bidez-Cumont, op. cit., II, 157.

[2] Ibid., 1. 10. 40-1; for the combination of "tragedy" and "myth" cf. Posidonius ap. Strab. 7. 3. 1 (Jacoby, op. cit., 2 A, F 104, p. 283. 5).

[3] Ibid., 1. 9. 26.

[4] O. Eissfeldt, *Ras Schamra und Sanchunjaton* (Halle, 1939), 67-71, 75-95; C. Clemen, *Die phönikische Religion nach Philo von Byblos* (*Mitteilungen der vorderasiatisch-aegyptischen Gesellschaft* 42, 3, Leipzig, 1939).

[5] Eusebius, *Praep. ev.* 1. 9. 24.

[6] Philo knew works of Hecataeus; he suggests that eulogies of the Jews ascribed to him cannot be genuine (Origen, *Contra Celsum* 1. 15).

[7] Cf. P. Meinhold in Pauly-Wissowa, *RE* XXI, 1685-7.

Christian equivalent of Philo's priests was responsible for corrupting the gospel.

The notion of primitive revelation, with or without interpolations, was so common in this period that we find semi-Christian gnostics using it as the foundation of their attempts to give allegorical explanations of the Christian books.

Among the Naassenes the true theology is both new and old. It is new in that it was supposedly contained in a tradition delivered by James, the Lord's brother, to a certain Mariamme;[1] it is old in that it was attested by the mysteries of the Assyrians, Phrygians, and Egyptians,[2] as well as those of Samothrace and Eleusis.[3] In the light of the theology one could explain a hymn belonging to the most ancient of all races, the Phrygians, as well as certain verses of the *Odyssey* and passages from the Old and New Testaments.[4]

Other gnostic books, including some discovered at Nag-Hammadi in Egypt, correlate Greek mythology and the Old Testament. According to Doresse, the fourth work in the unpublished Codex I has Eros in paradise before the creation of man; the first soul shed its blood on Eros, and the daughters of Pronoia became infatuated with him. In the fifth work, the *Exegesis on the Soul*, a citation from Hosea is followed by a reference to "the poet" (Homer) for the story of Odysseus and Calypso.[5] Presumably allusion was made to her offer of immortality if he would stay with her (*Odyss.* 7. 257).

This concern with primitive revelation was not confined to grammarians or gnostics. Among "orthodox" Middle Platonists there seems to have been concern only with the Greek antecedents of Plato.[6] But it is possible that Justin, so close in other respects to Middle Platonism, reflects some notion of an "ancient theology" when he describes philosophy as "sent down to men" (cf. Plato, *Tim.* 47 b) and originally one, before there were Platonists and even Pythagoreans (*Dial.* 2. 1).[7] Less orthodox Platonists noted the oriental sources of Plato's wisdom.

---

[1] Hippolytus, *Ref.* 5. 7. 1.

[2] Ibid., 5. 7. 20 (Wendland *ad loc.* refers to Cornutus, but as we have seen the notion was much more widely prevalent).

[3] Ibid., 5. 8. 9ff.   [4] For *Odyss.* 24. 2–10, cf. *Ref.* 5. 7. 30–41.

[5] J. Doresse in *Novum Testamentum* 1 (1956), 63–4. The combination of Hosea with Greek mythology recalls the system of Justin in Hippolytus, *Ref.* 5. 26. 34–5; 27. 4.

[6] Cf. Atticus in Eusebius, *Praep. ev.* 11. 2. 2–4.

[7] Cf. Cicero, *De orat.* 3. 61 (W. Schmid in *Hermeneia Regenbogen*, Heidelberg, 1952, 166).

Apuleius tells us that after Socrates' death Plato studied Pythagorean doctrine and then went to Egypt; he also wanted to visit the Indians and the Magi.[1] And Pythagoras was taught in Egypt by the Magi, especially Zoroaster, and later by Chaldaeans and Brahmans.[2]

The most famous Pythagorean-Platonist, the second century, however, was Numenius of Apamea.[3] He stated that "the tradition of Plato and Pythagoras is in accord with the traditions of the famous nations", the Brahmans, Jews, Magi, and Egyptians.[4] Presumably following Jewish sources, he identified Musaeus with Moses; and he also spoke of the ancient theologians. He says, for example, that "what the ancient theologians referred to Osiris and Typhon or to Dionysus and the Titans, Plato refers, because of piety, to the Athenians and the Atlantids".[5]

Numenius is a representative of a movement which traced back religious-minded Middle Platonism to oriental sources. Other examples include the contemporary pseudo-Egyptian *Hermetica* and the *Chaldaean Oracles*. And it is significant that the doctrine of the descent of souls from the Milky Way through the planetary circles first occurs in Numenius, the *Hermetica*, the *Chaldaean Oracles*, and in Celsus, where it is ascribed to the Mithraic mysteries.[6] Here is an example of the way in which new doctrines were treated as ancient.

In the second century this notion of a primitive Graeco-oriental theology comes to fullest expression in the *Alethes Logos* of Celsus, as Wifstrand, Chadwick, and Andresen have recently pointed out.[7] Against Jews and Christians Celsus appeals to the ancient theological tradition, handed down as *logos* by such theologians as Linus, Musaeus, Orpheus, Pherecydes, Zoroaster, and Pythagoras,[8] and as *nomos* by the most ancient nations such as Egyptians, Assyrians, Indians,

---

[1] *De Platone* 1. 3, p. 84 Thomas.

[2] *Florida* 15, p. 21 Helm; for ancient theology cf. *Met.* 11. 5.

[3] Cf. H. C. Puech in *Mélanges Bidez* (Brussels, 1936), 745–78; R. Beutler in Pauly-Wissowa, *RE Suppl.* VII, 664–78.

[4] E. A. Leemans, *Studie over den Wijsgeer Numenius van Apamea* (Brussels, 1937), 32 n. 3 (compares with Celsus).

[5] Ibid., T 51 (p. 112. 4).   [6] Ibid., p. 109. 5 and commentary.

[7] A. Wifstrand in *Bulletin de la société royale des lettres de Lund*, 1941–2, 396–404; H. Chadwick, *Origen Contra Celsum* (Cambridge, 1953), xvi; C. Andresen, *Logos und Nomos* (Berlin, 1955), 108–45.

[8] Origen, *Contra Celsum* 1. 16; others in 6. 42; 7. 28, 41.

Perians, Odrysians, Samothracians, Eleusinians, Hyperboreans, Galactophagi, Druids, and Getae.[1] These men and nations were "inspired".[2] But among Jews and Christians, as with their first leaders, there has been misunderstanding and deliberate distortion of this tradition.

Here we find much the same appeal to antiquity (*ubique et semper*) as in Plutarch, along with a theory of decline and fall like that of Posidonius or Philo of Byblos. We must ask, however, why Celsus includes the names he gives in these lists. It would appear that his concern is chiefly with the tradition centred in Orpheus and Pythagoras, and that of the two, Orpheus is the more important. Thus it was often held that Linus was the teacher of Orpheus, Musaeus his pupil.[3] Again, Pherecydes and Zoroaster were the teachers of Pythagoras.[4] As for the nations, we should normally expect to hear of Egyptians, Assyrians, Indians, and Persians, since these are the most famous peoples of the ancient east. What of the others? These too seem to be nations favoured by Orphic-Pythagorean tradition. Orpheus was king of the Odrysians,[5] and was initiated into the Samothracian mysteries.[6] He taught Eumolpus, who was said to have founded the Eleusinian mysteries.[7] Pythagoras was closely related to the Hyperboreans, Aristeas and Abaris.[8] I cannot find any relation between Orpheus or Pythagoras and the Galactophagi, but perhaps it is worth mentioning that Hecataeus had insisted that Hyperboreans and Getae were real peoples; Posidonius added the Galactophagi.[9] According to Alexander Polyhistor, Pythagoras has been instructed by the "Galatians",[10] and the Druids were famous not only for human sacrifice but also for philosophical theology, expressed in enigmatic form.[11] Zamolxis the Pythagorean had taught the doctrine of immortality to the Getae and had written their laws.[12] And Chadwick has noted that Celsus combined Pythagorean explanations with his description of the Persian mysteries.[13]

The true ancient doctrine for Celsus thus seems to be derived from

[1] Ibid., 1. 16; Chaldaeans and Magi in 6. 80.
[2] Ibid., 4. 36; 6. 17, 80; 7. 41; 8. 45.
[3] Cf. K. Ziegler in Pauly-Wissowa, *RE* XVIII 1, 1224–6.
[4] Bidez-Cumont, op. cit., II, 39–40.   [5] Ziegler, op. cit., 1236.
[6] Ibid., 1265–6.   [7] Ibid., 1266–7.   [8] Daebritz in *RE* IX, 269–70.
[9] Jacoby, op. cit., II A, F 103–4, 282–3.   [10] See p. 21 above.
[11] Diodorus Siculus 5. 31. 4.   [12] Iamblichus, *Vit. Pyth.* 173.
[13] Chadwick, op. cit., 335 n. 2.

Orpheus and Pythagoras—and behind them their oriental sources (Linus is said to have written Greek with Phoenician letters[1])—and transmitted through Greek poets and philosophers, especially Plato, whose *palaios logos* he apparently regarded as Orphic.[2]

In interpreting the writings in which this doctrine was transmitted, Celsus refers to the enigmatic speech employed by the ancients, such as the Egyptians, the Persians, Homer, and Heraclitus—indeed, by all ancient writers.[3] Christian gnostics have only "so-called enigmas".[4] The true enigmas can be understood by the exegete who has the true doctrine.

On the other hand, as in Cornutus, Plutarch, and Philo of Byblos, "allegory" is a term of abuse. The "more intelligent Jews and Christians" try to allegorize their books, but this is an impossible task, for the books themselves are exceedingly simple and straightforward, and those who allegorize them are therefore "forcing" the intention of the writers and producing allegories which are worse than myths.[5]

Celsus thus claims that his own exegesis of ancient writers is in harmony with their intention of handing down the truth in veiled form, to be uncovered by philosophical exegesis, while Jewish and Christian exegesis is merely defensive. Jews and Christians are trying to cover up the stupidity of the biblical writers.

We shall later see that Clement of Alexandria accepted the notion of a primitive Graeco-oriental theological tradition and made no attempt to refute Celsus. Now, however, we shall go on to the principal Neoplatonist adherent of ancient theology, in order to conclude this survey.

A generation or two later than Numenius and Celsus, the Pythagorean Platonist Porphyry of Tyre also expounded the notion of an ancient Graeco-oriental theology, first in his treatise *On the Philosophy from Oracles*, in which he uses oracular utterances both Greek and oriental. The primitive doctrine was revealed to Egyptians, Phoenicians, Chaldaeans (Assyrians), Lydians, and Hebrews, but corrupted by Greeks.[6] A possible reason for the corruption is given by Por-

---

[1] Diodorus Siculus; 3. 67. 1.
[2] Cf. Ziegler, op. cit., 1377–8; Andresen, op. cit., 113.
[3] Origen, *Contra Celsum* 3. 19; 6. 22; 6. 42.   [4] Ibid., 5. 64.
[5] Ibid., 1. 27; 4. 38, 49, 51, 87.
[6] Eusebius, *Praep. ev.* 14. 10. 4; cf. 4. 23. 2 (Egyptians and Phoenicians).

phyry's description of oracular utterances as not clear but enigmatic.[1] Similarly in his treatise *On Statues* he appeals to Orpheus and discusses the symbolic meaning not only of Greek gods but also of Attis, Adonis, and Egyptian deities.[2] The passage cited from Orpheus is interpreted as allegorical, and elsewhere Porphyry tells us that Orpheus spoke enigmatically.[3] So did Pythagoras, whose life Porphyry wrote;[4] so did Plato.[5] Indeed, all ancient writers indicated their theological views through enigmas.[6] Porphyry's treatise *On the Philosophy of Homer* is lost, as is that *On the Chaldaean Oracles*, but his book *On the Cave of the Nymphs in the Odyssey* shows the way in which his notion of an ancient theology made allegorical exegesis not only possible but necessary.

Naturally he knew that Pythagoras had studied with the Chaldaeans and indeed with Zaratus (Zoroaster),[7] and therefore when he tells us that he proved that the gnostic *Apocalypse of Zoroaster* was a forgery we must assume that his grounds were primarily theological.[8] He himself knew what the Magi had taught Pythagoras; this teaching existed in written form.[9]

In dealing with the question he may also have discussed chronology, for we know that in his *Chronicle* he pointed out that Thales, the first of the seven sages of Greece, flourished 123 years after the Chaldaean king Nebuchadnezzar.[10] And certainly in exposing another pseudepigraph he dealt with chronological questions. This was the book of the prophet Daniel, which he claimed was written by someone who was in Judaea in the time of Antiochus Epiphanes. The historical elements of Daniel were true; the prophetic elements were false,[11] or at least garbled. The "resurrection" refers metaphorically to Jews who hid in caves and came out after the victory of the Maccabees,[12] while the "time and times and half a time" are years (Dan. 12. 1–7).[13]

In thus dealing with pseudo-Zoroastrian and pseudo-prophetic

[1] Ibid., 4. 8. 2.   [2] Ibid., 3. 9. 2; 3. 11. 12–15, 43–51.
[3] Ibid., 3. 9. 4; *De antro nympharum* 16, p. 68 Nauck (ed. 2).
[4] *De vit. Pyth.* 41.   [5] *Hist. philos.* frag. 17, p. 14 Nauck.
[6] *De Styge*, frag. ap. Stob. *Ecl.* 2. 1. 19.
[7] *De vit. Pyth.* 12; Bidez-Cumont, op. cit. II, 37.
[8] *De vit. Plot.* 16; Bidez-Cumont, op. cit. II, 249–50.
[9] *De vit. Pyth.* 6; Bidez-Cumont, op. cit. II, 38.
[10] Jacoby, op. cit. II B (Berlin, 1929), F 1, p. 1198.
[11] Ibid., F 35, p. 1221.   [12] Ibid., F 57, p. 1228.   [13] Ibid., F 58.

29

books Porphyry was trying to keep pure the tradition of ancient wisdom by showing how those who were really alien to this tradition imitated its mysterious form.

The true tradition is to be understood only by those who know the underlying philosophical principles which are expressed enigmatically in it. Such exegetes are not allegorizing but are interpreting what is actually there. In the setting of this kind of exegesis of ancient documents, Hellenistic Jews and Christians worked out their own interpretations of their Bibles.

2

MOSES, THE PROPHETS, AND THE SPIRIT

HERETOFORE we have been concerned primarily with tracing the major ideas of inspiration and interpretation among Greek and Roman authors, and with showing, to some extent, the relation of inspiration to allegorization. We now turn to the way in which similar ideas were developed among Hellenistic Jewish authors who were concerned with these problems. Formally the results are much the same, as they will be much the same when we come to deal with Christian writers. The difference lies not in the method but in the presuppositions with which Stoics or Platonists or Jews or Christians begin.

Jewish writers naturally took the inspiration of Moses and the prophets for granted. Moses, the author of the Pentateuch, had spoken with God, and God had chosen him as the instrument through which the divine law was to be revealed. And the prophets themselves spoke of the word of the Lord which came to them. The Jewish community was a community whose life was centred in the revelation through Moses and the prophets.

The theoretical questions of inspiration and interpretation arose only when Greek-speaking Jews had produced the Septuagint, the traditional Greek translation of the Old Testament, and had confronted the Hellenistic world with its interest in theory. The earliest example we possess of Hellenistic Jewish exegesis of the Old Testament is probably the work of Aristobulus, at the end of the second century B.C. In his explanation of the Mosaic law we find the claim that Greek poets and philosophers used the Old Testament in a pre-Septuagintal Greek version, and that for this reason Greek philosophy agrees with Old Testament theology.[1] What Aristobulus really means is that by use of Stoic allegorization he can derive philosophy from the Old Testament. In his time Stoics had emphasized the power of God, and this he rightly finds in the creation narrative. He goes on, however, to explain that all the anthropomorphic allusions to God's voice, hands,

[1] Eusebius, *Praep. ev.* 13. 12.

31

THE LETTER AND THE SPIRIT

arm, face, feet, and walking about are figurative, as is the story of God's "descent" upon Sinai. They are to be taken "scientifically" (*physikōs*).[1] Proper understanding will bring the reader to marvel at the wisdom and the divine Spirit of God.

The kind of audience Aristobulus is addressing must be one which combined the *Timaeus* of Plato, with its stress on divine creative power, with Stoic allegorization. Such a combination certainly existed in his time, in the thought of such writers as Posidonius, and we can assume that Aristobulus is writing with such readers in mind. Like Stoic exegetes of Homer, he removes anthropomorphic expressions from his own inspired text.

Another example of allegorical exegesis among Hellenistic Jews is the treatise of Aristeas to Philocrates. Purporting to come from the third century B.C., it was actually written about 100. Aristeas holds that the Jewish scriptures are completely inspired. Nothing in them is either pointless or mythical. And their inspiration is not limited to the original texts. Aristeas describes the miraculous agreement found among the translations made by seventy-two translators in seventy-two days. Along with this strong doctrine of verbal inspiration goes a vigorous use of the allegorical method. The Jewish law is to be observed by Jews, but it contains a deeper, "natural" meaning (*physikos*, 171). For example, Moses was not concerned about mice and weasels when he gave the legislation; the laws were actually drawn up for the sake of justice and to promote contemplation. Since in the Stoic view man's relation with animals was not a matter for legislation and did not involve the question of justice, Moses must have been speaking of various kinds of men who are to be avoided (Lev. 11. 29).

Thus Aristeas insists on the inspiration of scripture in order to facilitate his adaptation of it to philosophy. The ultimate ground of knowledge lies in philosophy, of which the Old Testament is a symbolical expression.

Once the allegorical method had entered Hellenistic Jewish thought, it proved exceedingly useful. Of the Therapeutae, a Jewish ascetic group, Philo tells us (*Vit. cont.* 28–9) that they "allegorized the ancestral philosophy", since they believed that it contained symbols of "nature" hidden within the literal expressions. It was obviously

[1] Eusebius, *Praep. ev.* 8. 10. 1–17.

necessary for them to use allegorization if they were to find asceticism stressed in the Old Testament. Philo also says that they used books which contained these interpretations, and we may suspect that these books were among his sources.

Philo himself was the most prominent figure among Jewish allegorists. His significance lies not in his use of the method, for it was not new, but in the sheer volume of his writings, in his attempt to create a Jewish philosophical literature on the basis of Old Testament exegesis, and his later influence.

He had predecessors. These include the Therapeutae we have just mentioned, and probably others as well. He calls them "naturalists" or "scientific exegetes" (*physikoi* again). They have developed the Stoic method in relation to the Old Testament, and Philo associates himself with them (*Post.* 7). From them he takes the interpretation of Abraham as Mind and Sarah as Virtue; of the king of Egypt as Mind, the ruler of the body; and of Passover as either the purification of the soul or the creation of the world. On the other hand, they go too far when they introduce the Stoic Fate into Genesis or the Stoic cosmic conflagration into the doctrine of burnt offerings.

Philo tries to steer between too much allegorizing and not enough. He knows allegorizers who have advanced to the inner meaning of the law but have then stopped observing it, even though they try to remain within the Jewish community. Others have gone farther. They have become contemptuous of the law, and regard some of it as mythical or ridiculous. On the other hand, more literal-minded exegetes treated allegorization as "petty quibbling", a reproach which Philo uses in turn against them.

In his own exegesis he tries to combine loyalty to the presuppositions of scripture itself with the analogous statements to be found in the writings of Plato, Aristotle, and the Stoics. He values philosophy highly, but unlike the philosophers he does not place philosophical inspiration above that of the prophets. In his view the irrational inspiration of the prophets is beyond reason. This inspiration he describes as follows (*Spec.* 4. 49):

No pronouncement of a prophet is ever his own. He is an interpreter prompted by another in all his utterances, when knowing not what he does he is filled with inspiration, as the reason withdraws and surrenders the citadel of the soul to a new visitor and tenant, the divine spirit, which plays upon the vocal organism and dictates words which clearly express its prophetic message.

This spirit visits men periodically but does not remain with them, for in the Old Testament prophets we read that the word or the spirit of God "came upon" them and inspired them, only for a time. It remained with Moses for a long time, because of his virtuous nature. But it is essentially sporadic. It appears and works in states of ecstasy.

At one point Philo describes three forms of inspiration. These are (a) prediction through the divine spirit when the prophet is in an ecstatic state; (b) prediction or legislation by the divine voice (as at Sinai); and (c) prophecy through angels. For Philo the method of inspiration makes little difference. It is the fact of inspiration on which he insists.

It should be added that for Philo the Greek translation was also inspired, as it had to be since his exegesis was based on it. He says of the translators that "they prophesied as inspired men" (*Mos.* 2. 37), and calls them "not translators but priests and prophets" (2. 40). This language recalls Heraclitus' description of Homer, with its religious overtones. Like Heraclitus, Philo compares the understanding of his text with initiation into mysteries. His allegorical exegesis can be based on tradition, or on personal research, though such research leads only to conjecture. Ultimately Philo regards his own exegesis as inspired. A spiritual gift is necessary for the understanding of an inspired text.

How does Philo go about the work of exegesis? The details of his interpretation are often highly complicated, but his basic method is quite simple. It is based on his inherited Jewish faith in God as the creator and ruler of history, a faith which he expresses in terms taken from Greek philosophy. The biblical passages which correspond to this faith are taken literally, while others are allegorized. Thus Num. 23. 19: "God is not like a man", is a literal expression of truth, while Deut. 1. 31: "God is like a man", is adapted to the opinions of the multitudes" (*Immut.* 54). God is immutable (Ex. 2. 12); therefore passages ascribing passions to him must be allegorized. For though God is the creator he is not in any way anthropomorphic. Here Philo joins the philosophers. And his notion that there are some clear, literally true passages along with some inaccurate ones reminds us of Cornutus' explanation of Hesiod.

Philo believes that the literal meaning must be rejected if it involves something unworthy of God, when it leads to historical impossibility, or when the passage under consideration is itself plainly allegorical or symbolical. While these ideas were present in Stoic exegesis, we must note the basic difference between Philo and the Stoics. Since for him God was the active creator and miracle-worker, his idea of historical impossibility was different from theirs. He could accept as literally true passages which the Stoics would have taken allegorically. He claims to follow "rules" or "laws" of allegory, but he applies these rules on the basis of his theological presuppositions.

In the details of his exegetical work he comes close to rabbinic methods, partly because the rabbis had apparently been influenced by Greek grammarians, and partly because Philo himself was influenced by the rabbis. He holds that the exegete should look for an allegorical meaning when he finds any of the following difficulties:[1]

> Reduplicated expressions; seemingly superfluous words; tautologies; contradictory expressions placed close together; expressions apparently out of context; synonyms; plays on words; seemingly unusual adverbs, prepositions, or pronominal forms; compound words; ambiguous expressions; words whose meaning would change with a different accent or breathing; strange expressions generally; verbs used with inappropriate number or tense; verses or phrases in an unusual context; numbers, natural phenomena, and names which could have a symbolical meaning.

It is obvious that these problems have been raised as a result of grammatical study of the Greek Old Testament, and that many of them could be solved by recognition of difficulties either in the original Hebrew text or in the work of the translators. Indeed, many of the items in this list presumably reflect the criticism of the Old Testament presented by Greek grammarians, as Philo indicates from time to time.[2]

He cannot solve the problems by admitting the presence of errors in either Hebrew or Greek, since both texts are the product of divine

---

[1] C. Siegfried, *Philo von Alexandria als Ausleger des Alten Testaments* (Jena, 1875), 168–96.

[2] Cf. E. Stein, *Alttestamentliche Bibelkritik in der sp+thellenistischen Literatur* (Lwów, 1935), 4–10.

inspiration. He cannot trace a development in the biblical conception of God, since God is immutable. Only in the creation story in Genesis can he admit that there are non-historical elements in the narrative, and in his *Questions and Answers* he upholds historical reliability here as well. There is no merely historical interest in the biblical accounts,[1] but there is always history.

He therefore looks in the Pentateuch for an understanding of the meaning of human existence. In Genesis he finds the creation of two men. The first was ideal, heavenly, spiritual, generic. The second was mixed, earthly, fleshly, individual. This second man, Adam, was subject to the bond of sense-perception, which led him to the irrational passions of pleasure, desire, fear, and grief. On the other hand, the patriarchs are symbols of man's return to God. Abraham (Mind) passed through the study of nature (astrology) to logic and general education (symbolized by Hagar), and finally to ethics, the study of the highest good or virtue (symbolized by Sarah). By union with virtue he begot joy (Isaac). Moses passed through the same stages. He studied nature with the Egyptians, had a general Greek education, and finally achieved the vision of God. In short, Philo uses the lives of the patriarchs and of Moses to provide an outline of religious education in Hellenistic Judaism. Since Judaism is the true philosophy, this is the way to approach it.

These allegories of the patriarchs and Moses are ethical allegories which generally correspond to Stoic exegesis of the wanderings of Odysseus. Philo uses the Stoic words "physical" and "ethical" of his allegories, though he does not always observe a clear distinction between them. And just as the Stoics tried to find the moral law of nature in the texts with which they dealt, so Philo tries to find the universal law of nature which the patriarchs obeyed before the Mosaic law was given. This law was implanted in the world at creation. And since Abraham kept God's laws (Gen. 26. 5), this was the law he observed. A similar doctrine is found in rabbinic Judaism, with its notion of God's covenant with Noah and the legislation given then.

From natural law Philo goes on to defend the law of Moses on the ground that it was given by the Author of natural law. The law of Moses is in perfect harmony with the law of nature. It makes explicit

[1] *Somn.* I. 52.

what in nature is only implicit. All the Mosaic legislation has a basic rational meaning.

Thus on the basis of his philosophical theology Philo makes use of the allegorical method in order to correlate the "detached insights" of the Old Testament. He tries to fuse the Old Testament with an eclectic philosophical movement prominent at Alexandria in his times while retaining the cardinal Jewish principle of obedience to God's law.

Summing up Philo's idea of points at which the allegorical method can and must be applied, we find that these points all involve obscurities and instances of irrationality. On the one hand, they resemble the work of a poet; on the other, they are clearly produced by prophets writing or speaking in ecstasy, with their rational faculties suspended. Because of this suspension we find such peculiarities as inconsistency and bad grammar. Here Philo's doctrines of inspiration and interpretation flow together.

The peculiarities of scripture are due to the ecstatic state of the prophet, not to the immutable (and presumably grammatical and logical) God. The task of the exegete is to observe these peculiarities from a rational point of view and then to apply the allegorical method, also rational. The inspiration of the exegete is rational, not ecstatic.

The importance of Philo, at this point, is twofold: in the first place, he is the first Greek writer we know who so fully co-ordinates his theories of inspiration and interpretation and makes it possible to subordinate the varieties of biblical religion to a rational theology; and in the second place, he prepares the way for his Christian successors, Clement and Origen, who simply develop the theory based on Philo's practice, and (in Origen's case) make it more radical.

Philo's practice involves the sharp distinction between what Moses said and what he meant, for he is unwilling to accept an apparent lack of rationality in the Old Testament. This apparent irrationality is simply the form of the message. The rational content can be understood by the rational exegète who rewrites prophecy by using the allegorical method. Other exegetes, as Philo says, went farther and absolutely rejected the letter of the law. It may be that a record of their teaching has been transmitted to us (via Posidonius) by Strabo, as we have already seen. In this passage we find Moses described as a

critic of Egyptian and Greek idolatry and an exponent of Stoic pan-
theistic theology. Moses' temple had no images in it. It was a simple
shrine where believers could await dreams sent from God. No
festivals were associated with it. And Moses' earliest successors
remained faithful to the practice of righteousness and true religion.
Later, however, two kinds of error were introduced. Some Jewish
leaders were superstitious; they introduced dietary laws and circumcision. Others were tyrannical and brought in robbery (perhaps
temple taxes). In this way there was a decline from the purity of the
original legislation (see p. 20).

How much this account owes to Jewish sources and how much to
Posidonius must remain a matter of conjecture. We may suppose,
however, that the essential contrast between the pure legislation of
Moses and the additions made by his successors would have been
welcomed by allegorizers who were passing beyond observance of the
law. It would also provide some preparation for the Christian idea
that the law of circumcision and dietary observance was a later addition
to the core of revelation.

In first-century Judaism Philo was not alone in his belief that the
Old Testament contained allegory. Like him, Josephus firmly believed
in the inspiration of Moses and the other prophets. "In what Moses
said one might think one heard God speaking" (*Ant.* 4. 329). And all
the prophets described prior events by inspiration from God (*C. Ap.* 1.
37). The fulfilment of their prophecies proves their inspiration
(*Ant.* 10. 35, 79, 267). This inspiration apparently took place in
ecstasy, at least in the case of Balaam (*Ant.* 4. 118).

At the beginning of his *Jewish Antiquities* Josephus expresses his
agreement with the allegorizers (1. 24). In the Jewish law, he says,
there is nothing irrational or unbecoming either to the majesty of
God or to his love for mankind. It is entirely in harmony with the
nature of the universe, since Moses presented it partly in enigmas,
partly allegorically, and partly literally. Josephus is concerned far
more with history than with philosophy, as his works show us. But
he recognizes the validity and the importance of the allegorical
method, even though (like Philo) he criticizes the Greeks' attempts to
explain away the behaviour of the gods by allegorizing (*C. Ap.* 2. 255).

Generally speaking, Josephus' exegesis does not reflect the influence of Alexandrian allegorists. He is closer to the rabbis of Palestine, who were concerned primarily, though not exclusively, with legal rather than philosophical interpretation of the Old Testament. Out of the written law these rabbis derived the oral law which, so to speak, adapted the Jewish constitution to the altered circumstances of later times. The written law was what the rabbis said it was, for the tradition or oral law was often regarded as having an authority equal to that of the law given through Moses. It did not have authority in its own right, for only the Old Testament itself was divinely inspired. The exegete was only "building a fence" around the written law.

Rules of exegesis are ascribed to Hillel, a rabbi of the first century B.C. These rules may have come from Graeco-Roman grammarians and rhetoricians, as Daube has argued. In any case they were made necessary by the problems confronting Jewish teachers. These teachers wanted to claim some measure of rationality for their method. The rules are as follows: (1) "light to heavy", or *a fortiori*; (2) "equal judgement", or assimilation of various texts; (3) generalization from one text; (4) generalization from two texts; (5) correlation of general with particular; (6) parallelism in various texts; and (7) study of the context of a passage. These rules, essentially different from the principles of Philo, stress the resemblances and logicalities of scripture. But without some basic principle they would be useless. For this reason various rabbis attempted to find key principles in the law itself or in brief summaries. By means of such key principles the law could be interpreted. Thus we hear that Hillel told an inquirer that the key was the golden rule; the rest was only commentary.

At the beginning of our era, however, Judaism was not simply a static religion of legal observance. The Old Testament included not only the law but also the prophets and the (other) sacred writings. And in this period many Jews were looking forward to the coming of God's reign as foretold in prophecy. They began to interpret not only the prophetic writings but also other passages of scripture as predictive. Often they held that the last days would be like the first, and therefore described the last days in terms of the creation story in Genesis. Their emphasis on the Exodus as not only past but also future led them to interpret even the Song of Songs in Exodus terms.

Sometimes prophecy was regarded as already fulfilled. Josephus was not alone in believing that the predictions of the major prophets had already come true in the nation's history; and there were others who related prophecy not to the nation as a whole but to the sects to which they belonged. A notable example of this kind of interpretation has been found in the recently discovered Dead Sea Scrolls, especially in the Midrash on Habakkuk. "The explanation [of Hab. 2. 2] refers to the Teacher of Righteousness, to whom God made known all the secrets of the words of his servants the prophets." This teacher of righteousness was a Jewish sectarian leader apparently put to death in the second century B.C. His followers are often identified with the Essenes, whose exegesis was like that of the Dead Sea group.

Of the Essenes Josephus says (*Bell.* 2. 159) that "among them are those who profess to know future events; they are occupied with sacred books and various purifications and declarations of prophets". It would appear that they used the sacred books, including the law (for purifications) and the prophets, in order to produce their own predictions. If this is true, they probably made use of the same kind of exegesis we find in the Dead Sea books. This exegesis is what Wolfson has called "predictive allegory". It differs from the philosophical allegory used by Philo not so much in its method as in the purpose for which it is used. Philo wanted to find philosophy; the Essenes and others wanted to find predictions concerning themselves and their teachers. Both kinds of allegorization are based on the divine inspiration of scripture and the belief that its true meaning must agree with the exegete's own presuppositions.

Only among the informants of Posidonius and, it should be added, some Jewish "heretics" attacked in the book of Enoch (99. 2 and 104. 9–13)[1] is there any notion that the teaching of Moses has been interpolated.

[1] Cf. O. Cullmaun, *Le problème littéraire et historique du roman pseudo-clémentin* (Paris, 1930), 175, 186.

3

THE LAW AND THE GOSPEL

IN form, and to a considerable extent in content, the earliest Christian proclamation resembles that of the Jewish sects which we have already discussed. The gospel of Jesus is summarized by the evangelist Mark in the words, "the time (predicted in prophecy) is fulfilled, and the reign of God is at hand" (Mark 1. 15). This note of fulfilment, of standing in the last times, runs through the teaching of Jesus.

Belief in the fulfilment of prophecy implies belief in the inspiration of the prophets. And it is plain from Jesus' message as a whole that he accepted the inspiration of the Old Testament. The Psalms were obviously inspired, since David spoke "in the Holy Spirit" (Mark 12. 36). But Jesus himself was inspired by the Spirit (Mark 3. 29, 30), and because of his authority he could make distinctions within the law delivered by Moses. In one regard he did not go beyond the teaching of the rabbis, who found key passages which summarized the law. Jesus found this key in the double commandment of love toward God and toward one's neighbour (Mark 12. 28–34), or according to Luke (10. 25–8) he agreed with a lawyer that this was the key. In another regard, however, he went beyond the rabbis and differentiated the pure original law of God from additions made in the course of the tradition, beginning with Moses himself. Moses had permitted divorce because of the people's hard-heartedness. In God's original plan, however, there was no place for divorce (Mark 10. 2–9).[1]

From the time of Moses, then, additions were made to the pure law of God, and these additions were characteristic of the teaching of scribes and Pharisees. They "teach for doctrines the commandments of men and set aside the commandment of God", especially in regard to dietary regulations (Mark 7. 7, 8).[2] They "invalidate the word of God through their tradition" (Mark 7. 13). But Jesus regarded the process of invalidation as having begun, to some extent, with Moses himself. Deut. 24. 1, 2 was inserted as a concession to the people. It did not represent the will of God.[3]

[1] Cf. Mal. 3. 14–16.   [2] Based on Isa. 29. 13.
[3] W. G. Kümmel in *ZNW* 33 (1934), 124.

Again, in discussing the conflict between a vow to God and the duty of honouring father and mother as set forth in the fifth commandment, Jesus upheld the latter, in contradiction of the law on vows expressed in Deut. 23. 21–3.

Thus Jesus clearly rejected parts of the traditional law on the basis of his own authority, an authority reflected in such expressions as "You have heard . . . but I say to you" (Matt. 5. 21, 22, etc.) and in Mark's statement that "he was teaching them as one with authority, not as the scribes" (1. 22). This is not to say that he rejected the tradition and retained the law; as Kümmel points out, in Judaism the notion of law was always imbedded in the broader notion of tradition.[1] Jesus rejected either written or oral law when it did not correspond to God's will.

Where was God's will to be found? Certainly there were parts of the Old Testament in which it was set forth. The commandments on which everything else depended were stated in Deuteronomy (the Shema, 6. 4, 5) and Leviticus (19. 18). The commandments of the decalogue, or most of them, were premanently binding (Mark 10. 19; Matt. 5. 21–30).[2] The will of God in regard to monogamy can be discovered in the creation stories of Genesis (1. 27; 2. 24). And Jesus clearly regarded the stories of Noah and of Sodom and Gomorrah as divine warnings to his own generation.[3] Above all, he appealed to the teaching of the prophets, especially Isaiah, the minor prophets, and Daniel.[4] In their proclamations the will of God was expressed.

Yet Jesus was not primarily an exegete of the Old Testament. He was a messenger of God greater than Jonah or Solomon (Matt. 12. 41, 42). Like the prophets, he expressed the will of God directly, and like them he used parables.

The parable or *mashal* was a favourite mode of religious expression among the rabbis. It was a story involving an important correlation, at one or more points, with the religious orality to be conveyed. Jülicher argued that the parable had one and only one point, and thus could be distinguished sharply from allegory. Later critics have found parable and allegory not so distinct. Others have held that a parable

---

[1] W. G. Kümmel in *ZNW* 33 (1934), 110.   [2] R. M. Grant in *HTR* 40 (1947), 2–4.
[3] Matt. 10. 15; 11. 23, 24; 24. 37–9; Luke 10. 12; 17. 26–32.
[4] J. Hänel, *Der Schriftbegriff Jesu* (Gütersloh, 1919), 191–7.

is a story which stands up as a story apart from its correlative meaning, while an allegory is not independent in this way. Their distinction too is untenable. Both parable and allegory are forms of metaphorical language; the difference is one of degree rather than of kind. Allegory corresponds at more points than parable does to the ulterior meaning being conveyed. An allegory is a more complicated parable. The dividing-line is hard to draw.[1]

Modern critics have often suggested that the parables of Jesus are crystal-clear enunciations of moral truths. They have remembered the Prodigal Son and the Good Samaritan while forgetting the more difficult and obscure parables. Generally speaking, a Greek reader confronted by such a parable as the Unjust Judge would be convinced that a deep allegorical meaning lay behind it. And in fact the gospels tell us that Jesus provided explanations for some of his parables; Mark (4. 34) says that he explained all of them. There is no cogent reason for denying that he provided explanations at least for some.

Do we have his explanations? No doubt the tradition of these explanations, like the rest of the tradition of his sayings, has been somewhat modified in transmission. But in view of the fact, proved by Heinemann and others, that Jewish teachers in Palestine used allegorical exegesis, it is hard to deny absolutely that the one example given by all three synoptic evangelists is genuine. This concerns the parable of the Sower (Mark 4. 21–30 and parallels). The Sower sowed seeds in four places: (1) by the road, where birds ate them; (2) on stony ground, where they were scorched by the sun; (3) among thorns, which choked them; and (4) in good earth. To the disciples Jesus explains that the "birds" mean Satan; the "sun" means tribulation or persecution; and the "thorns" are the cares of the world, the deceitfulness of riches, and other desires. This explanation does not go much beyond the parable itself, and it need not be the creation of later tradition.

On the other hand, Mark has inserted between the parable and its explanation a statement which does not necessarily belong in this context. Jesus says to his disciples: "To you is given the mystery" (secret, as in the Dead Sea Midrash on Habakkuk) "of the kingdom of God, but to those outside everything takes place in parables." Here

[1] Cf. J. Pirot, *Paraboles et allégories évangéliques* (Paris, 1949).

the word "parable" means "enigma", in the sense of "enigmatic event". It must be the later tradition which has taken this saying and used it as a clue to the meaning of parables, since it is not really related to its context.

In the gospel of Matthew we find an explanation which clearly transforms a parable already close to allegory entirely into allegory. This explanation concerns the parable of the Tares (Matt. 13. 24–30). A man sows good seed in his field, but his enemy secretly sows tares in the same field. Grain and tares cannot be separated until the harvest; then the reapers will prepare the tares for burning and the grain for the barn. According to the explanation (Matt. 13. 36–43), the "sower" is the Son of Man, the "field" is the world, the "good seeds" are sons of the kingdom, the "tares" are the sons of the evil one, the "enemy" is the devil, the "harvest" is the end of the world, and the "reapers" are the angels. Does this explanation go back to Jesus? It is more likely that it is the creation of some early Christian exegete. And it provides a bridge to the gnostic exegesis we shall later discuss when it identifies "good seeds" with true Christians.

One more parable should be considered at this point. This is found in Mark 12. 1–9, and parallels. It is the story of a man who planted a vineyard and rented it to tenant-farmers. Various rent-collectors he sent were beaten or killed, and finally he sent his son. The tenants killed him in the erroneous belief that they would thus acquire the vineyard for themselves. "What will the lord of the vineyard do? He will come and destroy the farmers and will give the vineyard to others." This "parable" is certainly not a simple one-point parable. It is based on the allegory of Israel as a vineyard in the fifth chapter of Isaiah, and the allegory is developed in order to include Israel's rejection of the prophets and Jesus. The notion that to kill the heir means to obtain his inheritance seems artificial, and the parable may well be the creation of early Christians who were trying to explain what Jesus' death meant to the old Israel.

The teaching of Jesus, then, contains mysterious parables, both acted and spoken. These parables come close to allegory. But it was probably the early Church which developed complete allegorical explanations of the parables, along with the theory that parabolic teaching was used for concealment. The theory is more fully worked out in the gospel of John, where Jesus addresses allegorical parables not only to the Pharisees (ch. 10) but also to his own disciples (15. 1–10). Only toward the end does he speak not in parables but "openly" (16. 25, 29).

In the gospel of John, Jesus shows his opponents what the Old Testament means as prophecy. He tells the Jews that if they believed Moses they would believe him, for Moses wrote of him (5. 46). Perhaps John has in mind Moses' prediction of the coming of the true prophet (Deut. 18. 15). Again, Abraham was given prophetic vision of the "day" of Jesus; he saw it and rejoiced (8. 56). This verse may allude to God's promise of the birth of Isaac (Gen. 17. 17). And finally John comments that Isaiah could predict the coming of Jesus because "he beheld his glory and spoke concerning him" (12. 41); here he must be thinking of the vision of God's glory in Isa. 6. 1–3. In John we find Christian reflection on the meaning of Christ in the Old Testament. The inspiration of Moses and the prophets means that they learned of Jesus and hinted at his coming. The Christian exegete is the only one who can recover their true meaning.

The gospel of Luke similarly ascribes Christian exegesis to Jesus, especially after his resurrection, when he made this method clear to his disciples. On the road to Emmaus he reproached two disciples for their lack of understanding. The prophets clearly predicted that the Messiah had to suffer and only then enter into his glory. "Beginning from Moses and all the prophets he interpreted the predictions about himself in all the scriptures" (24. 27). "He opened the scriptures" (24. 32). These verses seem to imply that this kind of understanding of the Old Testament was a post-resurrection product. Again, in Jerusalem he reminded the disciples that everything written about him in the law of Moses, the prophets, and the Psalms had to be fulfilled. "He opened their minds to understand the scriptures", showing them that they could find predictions of a suffering Messiah, a resurrection on the third day, and the universal proclamation of the remission of sins (24. 44–7).[1]

The idea that these interpretations were given in or near Jerusalem may perhaps reflect the historical fact that such exegesis was the

---

[1] On this doctrine as the climax of Luke's last chapter cf. P. Schubert in *Neutestamentliche Studien für Rudolf Bultmann* (Berlin, 1954), 174–7.

contribution of the early Church of Jerusalem. Based to a considerable extent on Jesus' own approach to the Old Testament, it goes beyond it to seek for correspondences between his life and the Mosaic law (treated as prophecy). It is a kind of exegesis which inevitably led to allegorization.

We see examples of the exegesis of the early Jerusalem Church in the book of Acts. Like other Jews and Christians, the "saints in Jerusalem" firmly believed in the inspiration of the Old Testament, as we see for example in Acts 1. 16, a reference to a prophecy spoken by the Holy Spirit "by the mouth of David". They believed that the divine prophecies had been fulfilled. Some questions arose, however. Which of the prophecies really referred to Jesus and his followers? Jewish opponents of the Christians strongly doubted that the prophecies had been fulfilled in this way.

The earliest Christians seem to have had collections of texts which proved that the Messiah was Jesus. Of course they were not limited to the use of these texts alone. But since such "testimony books" existed among the Dead Sea sectarians, we may suppose that the Christians either used books already at hand or compiled their own. Passages doubtless caught their attention as they read the Old Testament, "searching the scriptures".

How were they to prove that such texts referred to Jesus and not to someone else? Did not the Psalms, for example, really refer to David? This problem is discussed in Acts 2. 29–35, and 13. 35, 36. The second Psalm says that God will not leave "my" soul in Hades or allow his holy one to see corruption. David cannot be referring to himself, for he died and was buried; he saw corruption; his tomb is still in existence. Therefore the Psalm refers not to him but to Jesus, who fulfilled the prophecy. Again, the 110th Psalm says to someone, "Sit at my right hand". This cannot mean David, who did not ascend into the heavens. In David's time the prophecy remained unfulfilled, and it therefore refers to Jesus.

The story of Philip and the Ethiopian eunuch (Acts 8. 27–35) deals with the same point. The eunuch is reading Isaiah aloud, and Philip asks him if he understands what he is reading. "How can I," asked the eunuch, "unless someone guides me?" After Philip joins him, the eunuch asks whether in Isa. 53 the prophet is speaking about himself or about someone else. Philip proceeds to show that the passage is a prophecy fulfilled only in the sufferings and resurrection of Jesus.

This, then, is the method which the early Church had developed before the time when the gentile mission was seriously undertaken. It is a method which supported the apostolic preaching with proofs from the Old Testament. It is a method which we see reflected in Paul's description of this preaching (1 Cor. 15. 3, 4). From the tradition he had received the conviction that Christ's death for men's sins was "according to the scriptures", as was his resurrection on the third day. Proof that the scriptures referred to Christ was provided by the method we have been discussing.

Among the "Hellenists" of the Jerusalem Church we find a bolder exegesis. This is exemplified in Stephen's speech in the seventh chapter of Acts. Stephen goes through the whole course of Jewish history from Abraham to Solomon and the prophets after him, and argues that the Jewish people always rejected their leaders and failed to understand the commandments which God (or the angels) gave them. This interpretation is based on a combination of the prophetic rebukes of the people and the Christian criticism of Jesus' rejection. Its importance for exegesis lies in the notion that while the Jews had received the law they did not understand it. Only Christians are able to comprehend its real meaning.

Only when we come to the letters of the apostle Paul, however, do we find a thoroughgoing reinterpretation of the Old Testament along Christian lines. It was Paul who provided most of the detached exegetical insights which later interpreters tried to systematize. And in his thought we see combined the various lines of exegesis which existed before him. He was thoroughly at home in the world of Jewish rabbinic exegesis and apparently knew something of allegorization as well. Along with these methods, both of which he probably knew before his conversion, he came to regard the Old Testament as a Christian book when he became a Christian, and thus "baptized" into Christianity the exegesis he had known.

His exegetical principles are most clearly set forth in two of his letters which were written about the years 53 or 54. These are Galatians and Second Corinthians, both written against Jewish Christians who still valued the law as law more highly than he did.

The first two chapters of Galatians set forth Paul's freedom in relation to Jewish Christianity and express his gospel in summary terms. In the third and fourth chapters he tries to find freedom foreshadowed in the law; he tries to prove that the Old Testament is essentially not law but gospel. This is a difficult point to prove, and he uses three methods to prove it. First he allegorizes; next he gives historical analysis; and finally he uses analogies. He begins with the famous example of Abraham as the example of life in faith. Abraham was accepted by God because of his faith, not because of his works.

As we have seen, Abraham was already regarded by Hellenistic Jews as the prime example of the man who is converted from gentile astrology and polytheism (since he once lived in Ur of the Chaldees) and comes to Jewish monotheism. We may well suppose that when Paul preached the gospel to the Galatians he used Abraham's faith as a prototype of the Galatians' own turning to God. Now he further develops the analogy, using Abraham's faith-righteousness as contrasted with the work-righteousness of the law. Here Paul goes beyond Hellenistic Judaism. Philo had assumed that Abraham's faith was naturally expressed in works of piety. Paul does not mention such works, for he is insisting on the importance of faith alone. He also refrains from mentioning the fact that Abraham became circumcised. This point would have been fatal to his argument.[1]

Later on in the letter he makes an even more determined attempt to use the figure of Abraham as a symbol. The result is the most elaborate allegory in his letters. He knows what he is doing: he explicitly states that the story of Abraham's wives and sons is "allegorical" (*allegoroumena*). Thus he is following a line like that taken by Philo, who had already distinguished the descendants of Hagar (the special legislation of the Jews) from those of Sarah (the essential law of nature).

Paul's interpretation differs from that of Philo only because it is Christian. Hagar was a slave; she represents Sinai, the law, the flesh, the present (earthly) Jerusalem. Her descendants, the Jews, are slaves. Sarah, on the other hand, was free; she represents the promise to Abraham, faith, the Spirit, the Jerusalem above. Her descendants, the Christians, are free. And since in rabbinic legend Isaac, the son of Sarah, was persecuted by Ishmael, the son of Hagar, this persecution

[1] By the time he writes Rom. 4. 11 he has solved the difficulty.

wás a prototype of Jewish persecution of Christians. What Paul has done is to take the exegesis of the Hellenistic synagogue and develop it along Christian lines.

He assumes that the Galatians will find his method congenial. "Tell me," he says to them, "you who wish to be under the law, do you not hear the law?" Then he proceeds from "it is written" to "these things are allegorical" without any apologies whatever. The allegorical method, he assumes, is as self-evident to his readers as it is to him.

At other points in the letter he uses a slightly more historical kind of analysis. For example, he argues that the law literally laid a curse on those who did not obey every detail of the legislation. Then he points to a text which speaks of another curse laid on everyone "who hangs on a tree". To the latter text he gives a symbolical meaning. Philo had taken the tree to mean "perishable matter", since in Greek *hylé* means both wood and matter. Paul refers it to the cross of Christ. And by identifying the two curses he finds that Jesus took on himself the curse originally laid on disobedient mankind. Here Paul combines allegory with history. He may also be reinterpreting a text used against Christians by Jews. It is hard to believe that Christians were the first to point to a text cursing their Lord. Paul probably found this text used by opponents of Christianity and revalued it by placing it in a theological, allegorical context.

At another point he lays more emphasis on history. He is trying to explain the relation of God's promise to Abraham and the Mosaic legislation, given 430 years later. We need not go into the details of this explanation, which Paul works out by using the analogies of a will and a codicil and of a minor's coming of age. The significant point is that here Paul seems to be using a historical theory not unlike that apparently found among Hellenistic Jewish allegorists. These theorists, as we have seen, believed that after Moses' time the law was corrupted; circumcision and dietary laws were added. Paul places the corruption earlier. It was Moses himself who made the additions (as in Jesus' discussion of divorce).

All these examples of exegesis are focused on one point. The law as law is no longer valid for Christians. It has a symbolical meaning. It is essentially prophecy, to be understood by use of the allegorical method. The same kind of interpretation is to be found in some of

Paul's other letters. For example, in 1 Cor. 9. 9, 10, Paul discusses the meaning of the Mosaic commandment not to muzzle an ox when it is treading out grain (Deut. 25. 4). "Is God", he asks, "concerned with oxen?" The context in Deuteronomy deals entirely with human beings, and Paul therefore assumes that this verse has an allegorical meaning. "It was written on our account."

In treating historical persons as examples or prototypes, Paul does not deny their historical reality. The promise of God to Abraham was not written *solely* on Abraham's account, but also on ours (Rom. 4. 23, 24). The events of the Exodus, which in Paul's view were prefigurations of a "new Exodus" in Christ, actually took place. They were written down for our instruction, since the ends of the ages have come upon us (1 Cor. 10. 11). There was a reciprocal correspondence between these two groups of events. Thus Paul could speak of Christ as "our Passover" (1 Cor. 5. 7), and could refer to the ancient Israelites as sharing in baptism and the Eucharist and drinking water from Christ, the spiritual rock (1 Cor. 10. 1–4). This kind of exegesis involves treating the Old Testament as predictive allegory, even though the historical reality of the events concerned is not denied.

Does it rest on a cyclical view of history, as Bultmann has argued? In a way it is true that events are regarded as repeating themselves. But there is a difference between the first event and the second. For Paul, Christ is certainly a second Adam (1 Cor. 15. 45–7), and Adam is a prefiguration (*typos*) of the one who was to come (Rom. 5. 14). The correspondence is not as important as the difference. Both Adam and Christ institute new beginnings, but Adam's disobedience resulted in sin and death, while Christ's obedience resulted in righteousness and life. History does not repeat itself, or even go around to the same starting point. These are two "creations", the old and the new, on a broken but relatively straight line.

How does Paul know what he knows? In other words, what is the ultimate principle of his exegesis? The answer to this question is found in Paul's conception of the spiritual meaning of the law (and the prophets). The Old Testament contains the oracles of God. And Paul, inspired by the same Spirit, is able to understand the spiritual meaning of the Old Testament (1 Cor. 7. 40; 2. 10–16). He makes this point plain in his second letter to the Corinthians. Christians are ministers of a new covenant, "not of letter but of spirit; for the letter kills, but the spirit [Spirit] makes alive" (2 Cor. 3. 6). By "letter" Paul seems to mean the literal, verbal meaning of scripture. He goes on to argue, by an analogy with a story about Moses, that Jews have never been able to understand the true meaning of the Mosaic legislation, because "even now whenever Moses is read a veil lies over their heart". On the other hand, "whenever a man turns to the Lord, the veil is taken away". Who is "the Lord"? The Lord, says Paul, means the Spirit, "and where the Lord's Spirit is, there is [exegetical] freedom". In other words, the only way to understand the Old Testament is under the guidance of the Holy Spirit, who removes the veil of literal legalism from the minds of believers. This Spirit gives exegetical freedom. He destroys the tyranny of words. He makes possible a Christian exegesis of the Old Testament, intuitive rather than based on words. Paul's distinction between "letter" and "spirit", as Cohen has pointed out, is not unlike that made by Philo and others between literal and true meaning.[1] But Paul has in mind especially the guidance of the Spirit of God which guides the interpreter. Philo too, as we have said, believes that his exegesis is inspired, but for him the Spirit does not have the importance it has for Paul.

Philo does not usually reflect the exegetical boldness we find in Paul. He cannot rewrite such a passage as Deut. 30. 12–14, which proclaims the availability and practicability of the law. "It is not in heaven, so that you might say, 'Who will go up to heaven for us and bring it to us so that we may hear it and do it?' It is not beyond the deep, so that you might say, 'Who will descend into the deep and bring it to us so that we may hear it and do it?' The word is near you, in your mouth and in your heart, so that you may do it." Paul, on the other hand, removes the context and reverses the content of the passage (Rom. 10. 5–10):

> Do not say in your heart, "Who will go up to heaven" (that is, to bring Christ down), or "Who will descend into the deep" (that is, to bring Christ up from the dead). What does it (scripture) say? "The word is near you, in your mouth and in your heart"—that is, the message of faith which we preach.

This is pure allegorization.

[1] B. Cohen in *Harvard Theological Review* 47 (1954), 197–203.

Is it possible to find anything like a system underlying Paul's "detached insights"? In other words, is it possible to tell what passages he would be likely to take literally and which he would allegorize? Perhaps we can find fragments which could fit into a system if we start from this exegesis of Deut. 30. 12–14, where Paul clearly rejects the literal meaning.

In the book of Deuteronomy (5. 22) Paul could read that God added nothing to the decalogue, which after all had already been given in Ex. 20. On the other hand, he could read in Deut. 31. 19 that the "song of Moses" (Deut. 32) was directly inspired by God. He might then assume that the "second law" (*deuteros nomos*) contained in the intervening materials was an addition, "inserted to increase the transgression" (Rom. 5. 20; cf. 4. 15). Specific instances seem to prove that this was the case. In the earlier additions in Deuteronomy we read of sacrifices, food laws, and festivals; but all of these had been superseded or abrogated.[1]

From the synoptic tradition Paul could have known that the charge of false prophecy (Deut. 18. 20–2) had been brought against Jesus (Mark 14. 60, 65), and that Jesus had taught that the humanitarian legislation of Deut. 20. 5–7 (cf. 24. 5) was irrelevant compared with the demands of the Kingdom (Luke 14. 18–20; cf. 1 Cor. 7. 32, 33). The "eye for an eye" and "tooth for a tooth" (Deut. 19. 21) had been superseded by the traditional sayings of Jesus (Matt. 5. 38).

Deuteronomy's preference for the first-born (21. 15–17) had been abrogated by God's choice of Isaac and Jacob (cf. Rom. 9. 12, 13), and the accusation of a son as a glutton and drunkard had actually been levied against Jesus (Deut. 21. 18–21; Matt. 11. 19; Luke 7. 34).

Worse of all, Deuteronomy (21. 23, 24) speaks of a curse on anyone who is "hanged on a tree", and this curse had perhaps already been invoked by Jews against Jesus. At any rate, Paul has to explain it away, taking it literally and setting against it another curse found in Deut. 27. 26 (Gal. 3. 10–13). When Deuteronomy goes on to speak of oxen and similar matters, Paul can be sure that the literal meaning is meaningless (cf. 1 Cor. 9. 9). Deuteronomy also refused a place among the people of God to eunuchs (23. 1), but Christians were

---

[1] Rom. 3. 25; 1 Cor. 5. 7 (Christ's sacrifice); Rom. 14. 14, 20; 1 Cor. 8—10 (food laws); 1 Cor. 5. 7 (Christ our Passover).

already accepting them (Acts 8. 38; cf. Isa. 66. 4–5). The vows of Deuteronomy 23. 21–3 had been annulled by Jesus (Mark 7. 9–13).

The Deuteronomic divorce legislation had already been invalidated by Jesus as a Mosaic concession (Deut. 24. 1, 2; Mark 10. 5–12; 1 Cor. 7. 10), and Paul's own experience had taught him the badness of the forty-stripes penalty (Deut. 25. 1–3). The rabbinic reduction of the penalty to thirty-nine stripes (2 Cor. 11. 24) would diminish the injury only slightly. Insult was added by the formal recitation of verses from Deuteronomy.[1] Thus Paul could hardly fail to believe that, in the immediate context, remarks about oxen (Deut. 25. 4) must have a symbolic meaning (1 Cor. 9. 9). And Jesus had pointed out the ultimate irrelevance of the regulations about levirate marriage (Deut. 25. 5, 6; Mark 12. 18–25).

This whole secondary legislation was summed up in a curse on anyone who did not obey all of it (Deut. 27. 26; "the book of the law", Gal. 3. 10), and it was binding upon anyone who was circumcised (Gal. 5. 3). It brought "wrath and indignation" (Deut. 29. 23–8), "tribulation and anguish" (Deut. 28. 53–7) upon everyone who worked evil (Rom. 2. 8, 9). But Christ came to take away this curse. Therefore the statement about the ease of fulfilling the law refers to the story of Christ and the gospel of faith (Rom. 10. 5–10).

The secondary legislation must be what was "added on account of transgressions"—presumably those committed by the people in the wilderness—"ordained through angels" rather than by God himself, "by the hand of an intermediary" (Gal. 3. 19). It effected the wrath of God (Rom. 4. 15). Thus Moses was entrusted with "the ministry of condemnation" (2 Cor. 3. 9; cf. Deut. 27. 26). The only way to understand the hidden meaning of this legislation is by turning to the Lord (2 Cor. 3. 16) and recognizing that by Christ it has been emptied of literal meaning (2 Cor. 3. 14).

Passages which speak of God's wrath or his curses (Deut. 27–32) are to be taken literally as directed against the Jews, though some of them have a symbolical meaning for Christians. Other passages have been completely invalidated.[2]

---

[1] Mishnah, *Makkoth* 3. 14.

[2] For allusions to Deut. 32 cf. J. Munck, *Paulus und die Heilsgeschichte* (Copenhagen, 1954), 37. Other Deuteronomic passages have their meaning severely modified. "Turn

We cannot find any clear system in Paul's thought, but he provides a point of departure for later gnostic and orthodox theories of interpolation.[1]

Paul's theory is further developed in his letter to the Colossians. The mystery of the word of God was hidden from ages (aeons, a word later used by gnostics) and generations, but has now been made manifest to God's saints (Col. 1. 26, 27). The mystery is now understood by the Christian who reinterprets the Old Testament. The Jewish festivals described in it are simply a shadow of things to come; their true "body" or embodiment is Christ (2. 16, 17). And in Ephesians, a letter modelled after Colossians either by Paul or by a later Christian, we find an important allegorization of the marriage of Adam and Eve (5. 22–32). Adam is Christ; Eve is the Church. The author uses his symbolism to urge husbands to love their wives, "even as Christ loved the Church and gave himself to it". He calls this exegesis "a great mystery". It is one of the secrets hidden from prior generations and now revealed to the Spirit-guided exegete.

We have seen that in method and results Paul combines rabbinic with Hellenistic Jewish exegesis, using both elements to find his gospel in the Old Testament. A little later comes the Epistle to the Hebrews, which is still closer to Philo. The recent commentary of Père Spicq has restored Philo to his earlier position as one of the most important influences on Hebrews. In this work Spicq has traced Philonic influence in vocabulary, style, arguments, exegesis (in part), themes and schemes of thought, and ideas of psychology. Yet Spicq insists on contrasting Philo's allegorization with that of Hebrews. Philo's work is "bizarre and in bad taste"; that of Hebrews is "essentially theological and, more precisely, Christological".[2]

Is this precisely the distinction to be drawn? Philo's picture of Melchizedek, king of Salem, is remarkably similar to the one we see in Hebrews. Both are allegorizations. Is not the author of Hebrews an

---

to the Lord" (Deut. 4. 30; 30. 10) is combined with Ex. 34. 34 (2 Cor. 3. 16). "Two or three witnesses" (Deut. 19. 15) become two or three visits of Paul (2 Cor. 13. 1). And Deut. 29. 23 is combined with Isa. 29. 10 (Rom. 11. 8).

[1] Cf. G. Quispel, Ptolémée: Lettre à Flora (Paris, 1949), 17–23; R. H. Connolly, Didascalia Apostolorum (Oxford, 1929), lvii–lxix. In the Didascalia as in Paul it is difficult to define the "second legislation" (p. lxviii).

[2] C. Spicq, L'épître aux Hébreux I (Paris, 1952), 61.

allegorizer? Of the Holy of holies he says, "Concerning these matters it is not now the occasion to speak individually" (9. 5). "What allegorist", asks Spicq, "would have resisted the temptation to exploit the symbolism of these cult objects?"[1] The answer to his question is that the author of Hebrews is an allegorist who does resist, and says so.

The difference between Philo and Hebrews lies not in method but in purpose. Philo wants to find God and the soul; the author of Hebrews wants to find Jesus. In both cases the Old Testament is taken allegorically. The one finds philosophical allegory; the other finds predictive allegory, though at one point, as we shall see, prediction comes close to philosophy.

At the same time Hebrews uses methods found in earlier Christian exegesis. For instance, Psalm 95 urges the people to remember God's prediction that they would not enter into his rest. Did they enter into it in the time of Joshua? No, they did not, for David (later than Joshua) reminded them of the prediction. Therefore the prophecy was not fulfilled until Jesus came (Heb. 3. 7–4. 10). Again, since the sacrifices at the temple were annual they obviously were not final (10. 1–3); and, in fact, "it is impossible for the blood of bulls and goats to take away sins", as we know from Psalm 40. This Psalm must have been uttered not by David (who offered sacrifices) but by Christ (Heb. 10. 4–9). Such examples prove that "the law had a shadow of the good actions to come, not the substance of the actions" (10. 1). This is the kind of exegesis we find in the early sermons in Acts.

But when we go on to ask what the substance was, we come back toward Philo. The temple cultus in Jerusalem was only a copy and shadow of heavenly realities. We know this because God instructed Moses to "make all things after the pattern (*typos*)" shown him on Mount Sinai (8. 5, 6). The temple was therefore only a figure (*parabolé*) of future realities (9. 9), the "greater and more perfect tabernacle not made with hands, that is to say, not of this creation" (9. 11). The eternal reality, not only future but always existent, behind the symbols is what both Philo and Hebrews look for.

Spicq prefers to call the method of Hebrews "Christological parabolism", and he points to its description of Isaac's rescue from death

[1] Ibid., 62.

as a "parable" or comparison referring to the resurrection (11. 19). For Hebrews the whole Old Testament is a parable or *mashal* in the sense that it is a riddle.[1]

When we consider the ultimate source of the exegesis, however, we find once more that we are close both to Paul and to Philo. The exegete himself is inspired, and there is thus, as Spicq says, "a correlation between the inspiration of the Old Testament and that of the exegete".[2]

> He discovers, beyond the literal sense and the historical context, the profound meaning of scripture. By a religious intuition, he restores their true meaning to facts and to persons. . . . He discerns, he reads, a gospel latent in the Old Testament.

But the distinction between allegorization and "parabolism" or typology is essentially theological, not historical. Spicq's description could have been used by Philo to set forth the meaning of his own work.

If we turn from exegesis of the Old Testament to the inspiration of Christian writers themselves at the end of the first century, we find two different attitudes. On the one hand, the author of the Apocalypse clearly regards himself as ecstatically inspired. "I was in the Spirit on the Lord's day, and I heard behind me a voice as of a trumpet saying, 'Write what you see in a book and send it to the seven churches'" (1. 10, 11). His claim to inspiration is obvious in all his accounts of visions. It is made explicit at the end of his book where he lays a curse on anyone who adds to or subtracts from "the words of the prophecy of this book" (22. 18, 19). This curse reflects the one found in (Moses') Deuteronomy. He writes allegorically and symbolically and he believes that there is a "spiritual", allegorical meaning in the Old Testament (11. 9), which he understands.

On the other hand, the author of Luke–Acts thinks of himself as an historian, as he makes plain in the prefaces to his two volumes. In Acts the inspired apostles say, "It seemed good to the Holy Spirit and to us" (15. 28). In his own prologue the evangelist says simply, "It seemed good to me" (Luke 1. 3). Only in later manuscripts is a

---

[1] C. Spicq, *L'épître aux Hébreux* I (Paris, 1952), 61.
[2] Ibid., 349.

mention of the Holy Spirit added here. Luke is a recorder of tradition, and does not claim special inspiration.

Similarly the Fourth Evangelist lays emphasis on testimony, and speaks of signs not written down in his book. He is a collector of signs which will produce belief in Jesus as the Christ (20. 30, 31). Those who first used his book seem to have regarded him as a witness, not as an ecstatic figure. They added their comment that his testimony was true (21. 24). On the other hand, John undoubtedly shares in the gift of the Holy Spirit to the Church, and thus is guided into the whole truth (16. 13). But he has no special gift as an evangelist.

In the New Testament as in the Old, dreams, heavenly voices, and angelic visitors play a fairly prominent role as means of revelation. In arguing with the Galatians, the apostle Paul can claim that he did not receive his gospel from any human teacher; it came to him through revelation from Jesus Christ (Gal. 1. 12). He goes on to portray the nature of his former life in Judaism, a life which he implies could have been changed only by an agency outside himself (1. 13–16). Apparently he had been given further visions and revelations at various times (2 Cor. 12. 1–4, 6). And, inspired by the Spirit, he could speak in tongues more than any of his Corinthian converts could (1 Cor. 14. 18).

We have seen that the evangelists make no claim that their works are the product of divine inspiration. Paul makes such a claim only very tentatively and at one point (1 Cor. 7. 40). Like the evangelists, he is more of a witness, an apostle, than a prophet with a message directly from God. He is a witness to Jesus Christ, and the historical nature of the revelation in Christ calls for testimony rather than for inspiration, ecstatic or otherwise. While the whole Christian community is inspired by the Holy Spirit, especially in giving testimony to the gospel (cf. 1 Pet. 1. 12), only one New Testament writer, the apocalyptist John, explicitly claims that his writing is inspired.

4

THE SECOND CENTURY

INSPIRATION AND EXEGESIS IN THE APOSTOLIC FATHERS

AT the end of the first century and the beginning of the second, Christians were concerned with the question of inspiration. We have already seen that the author of the Apocalypse claims to be inspired. This claim is also made by some of the Apostolic Fathers. Clement of Rome, giving counsel to the Corinthians about 97, believes that his letter is inspired by the Holy Spirit (63. 2). Another Roman Christian, Hermas, explicitly ascribes his visions to the Spirit (*Vis.* 1. 1. 3) and to an old woman who at first seemed to be the Sibyl but was really the pre-existent Church (*Vis.* 2. 4. 1). His commandments were given him by a spiritual messenger or angel who was to remain with him permanently (*Vis.* 5. 2). The same messenger told him parables and explained some of them to him. Obviously Hermas regards the form and content of his books as inspired. He wrote them in obedience to angelic orders. He describes one of his visions as the reproduction of a mysterious book given him by the old woman (*Vis.* 2. 1. 3, 4). In Syria, Ignatius of Antioch does not suggest that his letters to the Churches are inspired, but he claims prophetic authority; he himself can speak with "God's voice" (*Philad.* 7). There is therefore at least the possibility that what he writes is inspired by the Spirit. And in similar fashion, "Barnabas" claims inspiration for his "gnosis", his way of dealing with the Old Testament, for it was given him by the Lord (5. 3). By implication the content of his letter is inspired.

The Apostolic Fathers regard the Old Testament as inspired. For Clement as for the apostle Paul, it is inspired by the Holy Spirit and can be called "the oracles of God". The "words of the Lord Jesus" clearly have an authority equal to that of the Old Testament (13. 1; 46. 7). And by implication the letters of Paul share this authority. "Christ is from God and the apostles are from Christ; therefore both proceed in order from the will of God" (42. 2). Since Clement's own letter is inspired by the Holy Spirit, *a fortiori* the apostle's letters are inspired too.

The inspiration of the prophets is discussed in the pseudonymous epistle called 1 Peter. Its author describes the prophets as inspired by the Spirit of Christ to foretell his sufferings and subsequent glory. This notion goes beyond earlier ideas, since 1 Peter relates the inspiration as well as the interpretation of the prophets to Christ. They themselves, he says, inquired about the time and circumstances in which their prophecy would be fulfilled, and it was revealed to them that the fulfilment would come not in their own time but later (1. 11, 12). In his letter the author quotes from Isaiah and the Psalms; presumably these are the prophecies he has in mind. For the prophets' inquiry he may be thinking of Isa. 53. 1: "Lord, who believed our report?" We know this verse was used by early Christians; it is quoted in Rom. 9. 16 and John 12. 38. What 1 Peter argues against is the Jewish notion that some of the prophecies were fulfilled long before the time of Jesus. The prophets themselves knew better.

Ignatius too regards the prophets as pre-Christian Christians. "The most divine prophets lived in accordance with Christ Jesus, inspired by his grace" (*Magn.* 8. 2). They were his disciples "in the Spirit" and expected him as their teacher. Since they waited for him in righteousness, he raised them from the dead at his coming (*Magn.* 9. 2; Matt. 27. 52?). Christians love them because their proclamations referred to the gospel and they set their hope on Christ (*Philad.* 5. 2). Ignatius knows Christians (?) who refuse to accept the gospel unless it can be confirmed by the Old Testament (*Philad.* 8. 2). To his statement, "It is written", they reply, "That is just the question". All he can say is that the key to the Old Testament is the gospel, not vice versa (cf. *Magn.* 10. 3; *Philad.* 6. 1). Because it was Christ's Spirit which inspired the prophets, only in Christ can the prophets be understood. Ignatius and 1 Peter agree.

When we consider the exegetical methods of the Apostolic Fathers, we find that of Clement very matter-of-fact. It can hardly be called exegesis, since his purpose in writing the Corinthians is entirely practical and he uses the Old Testament only as a storehouse of moral examples (*hypodeigmata*). He knows the method of predictive allegorization, however, for at one point (12. 7, 8) he refers to the scarlet thread of Rahab as a predictive sign and a prophecy which foretold redemption through the blood of the Lord. More extensive use of this method would have been alien to the spirit of his letter.

Among other writers a more imaginative exegesis is prominent. This is an exegesis which provides a bridge between earlier Christian treatment of the Old Testament as prophecy and the later speculations of gnostics. Ignatius, for example, discusses the three gospels he knows (Matthew, Luke, and John) in a manner at least intelligible to gnostics. In reworking the story of the star at Bethlehem, Ignatius treats the star as Jesus himself, suddenly appearing and disturbing the rulers of the heavenly regions (*Eph.* 19. 2, 3). He can do so because, as he elsewhere claims, he thoroughly understands the heavenly regions and the working of the powers in them (*Trall.* 5. 2). He also explains that Jesus was baptized "in order to purify the water" (*Eph.* 18. 2), even though he knows the Matthean explanation that it was "to fulfil all righteousness" (*Smyrn.* 1. 1). In reworking the Lucan account of the resurrection, he reports that Jesus said, "Handle me and see that I am not an incorporeal demon" (*Smyrn.* 3. 2, 3). This interprets Luke 24. 39 in terminology later used by gnostics. And when he describes the Lord's breathing the Spirit on the disciples (John 20. 22), he says that what the Lord breathed on them was "the odour of incorruption" (*Eph.* 17. 1). All these modifications or interpretations are paralleled in gnostic ideas later reported by Clement of Alexandria. Did Ignatius use gnostic expressions, or did the gnostics read Ignatius' letters? If they used his phrases, they must have done so because they found them congenial to their own views. In either case, Ignatius is translating the gospels into terminology at least acceptable to gnostics.

Secret gnosis appears again as the foundation of the exegetical method of the Epistle of Barnabas. As we have said, its author claims that his method comes from the Lord. And he uses it to prove that the Old Testament convenant, and the Old Testament itself, is not the property of both Jews and Christians. It belongs to Christians alone (4. 6, 7). He argues on the basis of the Old Testament prophecies that sacrifices and fasts were to be abandoned, and then turns to show that all the Jewish sacrificial practices were really prefigurations of the life and work of Jesus. The dietary laws were concerned with the avoidance not of animals but of men symbolized by the animals. "We who have rightly understood the commandments speak them as the Lord wished" (10. 12). On the other hand, baptism, the cross, and Jesus himself are often to be found in the Old Testament, since Christians are the true heirs of God's convenant. Moses did receive the tables of the law for the Jews, but they were not worthy to have them. Now the Sabbath has been replaced by the eighth day (Sunday), and the temple by the true and spiritual temple of Christians.

"Barnabas" tells us that nothing necessary for salvation has been omitted in his treatise. What of the method by which he reads the essentials into the Old Testament? As Windisch has noted, it is primarily Jewish, especially Hellenistic Jewish. The most exotic instance of exegetical wilfulness is found in the explanation of the number 318 (9. 8). Abraham had 318 servants, according to Gen. 14. 14. In Greek this is TIH. The T is the cross, and the IH the first two letters of Jesus' name ($IH\Sigma OY\Sigma$). Philo would have rejoiced in such a pupil, at least as far as the allegorical method is concerned.

The Epistle of Barnabas is apparently the reworking of lectures in a Christian school. But the use of such a method as we find in this epistle was not confined to schools. It occurs again in the homily (possibly from Rome) known as 2 Clement. Here there is no discussion of inspiration or of exegetical method, but there is a good deal of semi-gnostic allegorization. The homilist interprets Gen. 1. 26, 27 (God's creation of man in his image, male and female) as referring to the creation of Christ (the male) and the Church (the female). This exegesis reminds us of the marriage of Christ and the Church in Ephesians, and may well be based on Eph. 5. 25–9. But 2 Clement goes farther. The flesh corresponds to the Church and the spirit to Christ, and the flesh is an antitype of the spirit (14. 2–4). The homilist seems somewhat confused, and confusion is confounded when he brings in the Gospel of the Egyptians (12. 2–6). In this gospel the Saviour says that the two must become one and the inside as the outside. The homilist explains that what he means is that there must be one soul in two bodies and that the soul inside (female) must become as the body outside (male). Evidently "Clement" has in mind a list of semi-gnostic pairs (syzygies, the gnostics called them) and tries to relate them to Genesis and Egyptians, without much success.

In Asia Minor exegesis was more restrained. Polycarp and Papias did not regard their own writings as inspired. Polycarp recognized the difference between his own wisdom and that of "the blessed and glorious Paul" (*Phil.* 3. 2), and when he spoke of "the apostles and prophets who preached the gospel" (6. 3) he did not regard his inspiration as like theirs. Papias, like the authors of Ephesians and 2 Clement, allegorized the creation story of Genesis in terms of the Church, but his main concern was with the historical tradition of the Lord's deeds and words.

The importance of Papias' fragments lies in this stress on historical writing. Papias tells us that Mark wrote down the apostolic tradition as he remembered it, taking care not to omit anything of what he heard or to make erroneous statements. As Peter's "interpreter", he wrote in Greek. Matthew, on the other hand, composed the "logia" in Hebrew, and each reader had to translate as best he could (Eusebius, *H.E.* 3. 39. 15). Behind the gospels Papias found the "living and abiding voice" of oral tradition persisting into his own time (ibid., 4).

Thus for Papias the gospels represent historical tradition which can be found more authentically in unwritten form. His view left open the possibility that gnostic sects might claim higher authority for their own unwritten traditions. It also allowed for human error. Mark's memory might have been fallible. The translators of what Matthew wrote may not have been competent. And the apocalyptic tradition which he said came from the circle of the apostle John was not especially edifying. It described the miraculous productivity of grape-vines in the age to come. For all these reasons Papias' work was later largely neglected. The Church was entering a conflict not over the historical reliability of the gospels but over the inspiration and interpretation of the Old Testament and what came to be regarded as the New.

MARCION

This conflict was really a series of conflicts. First came the question of the place of the Old Testament, a question raised most forcefully by Marcion, who argued that the Old Testament had to be rejected since it contradicts the true gospel of Jesus and of Paul. When the Church sought refuge in its traditional allegorical method, it encountered the second question, posed especially by the Valentinians. These gnostics insisted that the gospel too should be taken allegorically, and that it really corresponded to their own theories of the aeons and of human nature. The Church then relied on its interpretation of the Old Testament as predictive rather than philosophical allegory, only to meet the third question, that of the Montanists. If the Old Testament was prophecy, so was the New. The predictions of a coming Paraclete were fulfilled in their leader Montanus. Out of these conflicts arose the Christian theology of the late second century.

Marcion came to Rome from Pontus shortly after the Jews had lost a bloody messianic war against the empire. Under these circumstances he expected a favourable reception for his rejection of the Old Testament. In his belief the highest God, completely unknown except in his self-revelation through Jesus, was to be distinguished from the Old Testament God, the God of the Jews, who had created the world and given the law. Through his prophets this Jewish God had predicted the coming of a warrior messiah—who had (obviously) not yet come, in spite of Jewish hopes. Jesus was not this Jewish messiah but a "saving spirit" who had descended to earth and had seemed to assume human flesh. His Jewish disciples had misunderstood his message. Only Paul, because of a special revelation, had known what it meant.

Marcion began his *Antitheses*, a collection of discrepancies between the Old Testament and the true gospel, with a Pauline proclamation of the uniqueness of the gospel.

> O miracle upon miracle, ecstasy, power and astonishment it is, that one can say nothing about it, nor think about it, nor compare it with anything.[1]

This proclamation suggests that Harnack may well have exaggerated the importance of Marcion's philological methods. Marcion's starting-point was this ecstatic statement about the miraculous nature of the gospel. The philological work was the consequence, not the cause. He had to explain how it was that the gospel had been distorted, and how it was that he could recover it.

[1] F. C. Burkitt in *Journal of Theological Studies* 30 (1928–9), 279–80.

Marcion apparently started his work by considering passages in Galatians and Romans in which Paul speaks of the uniqueness and truth of his gospel to the gentiles. What Paul meant was the unwritten true gospel, which was distorted and contradicted by Peter and other apostles. Harnack has argued that the original apostles were merely confused; they were not false teachers.[1] For this point he relies on Irenaeus' statement that in Marcion's opinion they proclaimed the gospel while still influenced by Jewish ideas.[2] But since Irenaeus also says that it was they who combined legalistic expressions with the words of the Saviour,[3] they can hardly be absolved from blame. They must be the ones who, in Tertullian's words, interpolated the gospel in order to include the law and the prophets.[4] Presumably their successors interpolated the Pauline epistles.[5]

Marcion's work of removing interpolations thus resembles that of his older contemporary Philo of Byblos, who recovered pure Phoenician mythology from the hands of allegorizing priests. Like Philo, he was determined to restore the pure religious tradition. Sometimes Marcion is regarded as a textual critic who reconstructed the authentic gospel on philological grounds, presumably actually possessing a non-interpolated Luke. But there is no evidence for the existence of such a document, for it can be demonstrated that the passages he deleted were those which contradicted his theology.[6] And in any case one can hardly deny the theological motivation of Philo and, for that matter, of his predecessor Cornutus. This kind of textual criticism is not necessarily characterized by pure objectivity.

To find out, or rather to prove, what Jesus taught, Marcion relied on his expurgated gospel, derived from the canonical Luke. By omitting the verses between Luke 3. 1 and 4. 28, he was able to show that Jesus "came down" to Capernaum in the fifteenth year of Tiberius Caesar—"came down" out of heaven.[7] Naturally he also omitted the first two chapters of Luke, which reveal that Luke writes not as an

[1] A. v. Harnack, *Marcion: das Evangelium vom fremden Gott* (ed. 2, Leipzig, 1924), 37–9.
[2] Irenaeus, *Adv. haer.* 3. 13. 2.　　[3] Ibid., 3. 2. 2.　　[4] *Adv. Marc.* 4. 4.
[5] Examples in Harnack, op. cit., 40*–176*.
[6] Evidence is provided in Appendix I.
[7] This exegesis (Harnack, op. cit., 183*—5*) was applied to Jesus' "descent" in John 2. 12 by the Valentinian Heracleon and taken over from him by Origen (J. Daniélou *Origène*, Paris, 1948, 191).

inspired poet or prophet but as an historian. These chapters also show that Jesus had a human mother. By making only a few more excisions, Marcion was able to show that Jesus spoke of his "mother" as "those who hear the word of God and do it" (Luke 8. 21). He also argued that Jesus' whole teaching was novel and proclaimed a novel God. He astonished synagogue worshippers by his teaching against the law and the prophets (Luke 4. 22; Marcion has deleted the actual content of his teaching). By touching a leper he broke the law (Luke 4. 40). To be one of his disciples he chose a tax-collector outside the law (5. 27). He rejected the teaching of John the Baptist, since it came from the Creator (5. 33), and in turn John was scandalized by him (7. 20). He overthrew the Sabbath (6. 1 ff.), and in his great Sermon set forth new regulations for human life.

From the evangelists' day the parables of Jesus had been treated as allegories, and Marcion was therefore free to interpret them in the same way. In Luke 11. 5–8, it is the highest God who opens to the unknown man knocking at the door. The enigmatic "leaven of the Pharisees" (12. 1) is their preaching of the Creator. The thief who comes in the night (12. 40) is the Creator. The man who sows the grain of mustard seed (13. 19) is either Christ or anyone who has the seed of the kingdom in the garden of his heart. The kingdom of God is like leaven (13. 21), not like unleavened bread, since the latter would refer to the Passover of the Creator. The "banquet" of Luke 14. 16 signifies a heavenly banquet of spiritual delight. In other words, it is to be taken spiritually rather than materially.

The impression made by Marcion's teaching at Rome is reflected in a story told two hundred years later by Epiphanius. He says that Marcion brought his exegesis to the attention of Roman presbyters by asking them to explain the meaning of Jesus' sayings about new wine in old wineskins and the patch on old clothing which results in a rent (Luke 5. 36, 37). The presbyters gave him exegesis which treated the sayings historically. The old wineskins were the hearts of the Pharisees and scribes, while the old clothing meant Judas, grown old in avarice, who could not be patched on to the garment of the apostles. Marcion vehemently rejected this kind of interpretation. It did not do justice to the newness of the gospel. It stressed historical continuity rather than the rejection of the law and the prophets. And when the presbyters decided not to accept him or his exegesis, he replied, "I will rend your Church and cast division into it for ever" (Epiphanius, *Pan. haer.* 42. 2). This story is at least symbolically true. Marcion believed that like Jesus he had come to bring not peace but a sword.

In order to make the lines of division clear, Marcion had to reject the allegorical method which Christians had been using in order to correlate the Old Testament with the gospel. His rejection, however, was not entirely consistent, as Tertullian pointed out (*Adv. Marc.* 3. 5), since he accepted Paul's allegorizations in 1 Corinthians, Galatians, and Ephesians. Later Marcionites tried to achieve consistency by changing "prefiguratively" in 1 Corinthians 10. 11, to "non-prefiguratively". Marcion himself apparently did not do so.

What answer could the Church give to this massive attack on its central doctrines? Justin and Irenaeus are our most important early witnesses. They insisted that there was one God who had revealed himself in both the Old Testament and the gospel. The Old Testament, therefore, had to be understood prophetically and allegorically in terms of the gospel. Irenaeus and Justin agreed that it could be understood only by virtue of a special gift of grace, and Irenaeus made it plain that this gift of grace was confined to the Church's teachers. He also developed the notion of a progressive revelation in order to answer Marcion's criticisms of Old Testament morality. Since the Church had four gospels, not just one, the four together confirmed its apostolic doctrines.

SYRIANS AND VALENTINIANS

Marcion was not the only person who threatened the exegetical security of the second-century Church, nor was he the only admirer of the apostle Paul. Our earliest account of the teaching of the Simonian gnostics shows clear traces of Pauline doctrine. Simon's followers were free to live as they pleased because "by grace"— Simon's—they were saved, not by works (Eph. 2. 8). The law and the prophecies were given by angels in order to enslave mankind, and these angels had made the world. Here Simonian doctrine seems to be based on Gal. 3. 19 (law given through angels) and 4. 9 (slavery to law and to elemental spirits). The Simonians took some Pauline verses, by implication dualistic, and pressed them into the service of a dualism far more consistent than Paul's.

Another early gnostic exegete was Saturninus of Antioch, who interpreted the "Let us make" of Gen. 1. 26, as addressed by the God of the Jews to other angels, and the "in the image" as referring to a luminous image which descended from the unknown God above. Thus Saturninus explained both the badness of man's physical existence and the goodness of the divine spark, later inserted into Adam. How could he justify this rewriting of the Old Testament? He held that some of the prophecies were spoken by the angels who made the world, others by Satan, the adversary of the God of the Jews. By thus ascribing the prophets' inspiration to various angels, however, Saturninus did not explain the source of his own knowledge. But if we fill in this gap from the *Apocryphon of John*, a gnostic document very close to his circle, we find that true *gnosis* came from Jesus, the emissary of the unknown God; it was transmitted to the apostle John, the only apostle who understood Jesus' teaching. The *Apocryphon's* John is the equivalent of Marcion's Paul.

We do not know how Saturninus distributed the Old Testament among the various angels. Irenaeus, however, tells us something of the Ophites' doctrine of inspiration, and these Ophites too were close to the *Apocryphon*. They held that as there were seven planetary angels, so there were seven groups of prophets, each inspired by one angel. The distribution seems to have been confused by Ophites, by Irenaeus, or by later copyists. And when Preuschen tried to improve it, it cannot be said that he succeeded.

ANGEL	PROPHETS (Irenaeus)	PROPHET (Preuschen)
Ialdabaoth	Moses, Joshua, Amos, Habakkuk	Moses
Iao	Samuel, Nathan, Jonah, Micah	Joshua
Sabaoth	Elijah, Joel, Zechariah	Samuel
Adonai	Isaiah, Ezekiel, Jeremiah, Daniel	Nathan
Eloi	Tobias, Haggai	Elijah
Orei	Micah (!), Nahum	Tobias
Astanfei	Ezra, Zephaniah	Ezra

Ialdabaoth is the God of the Jews; hence he inspired Moses and Moses' successor. Iao is evidently Yahweh, and the Old Testament tells us that Samuel, Nathan, and Jonah were his prophets. Sabaoth is frequently mentioned by Zechariah, as well as once by Elijah (1 Kings 19. 10). Adonai is named by Isaiah (8. 7) and often by Ezekiel. The last three angles are harder to correlate with the prophets. Elohim (or the "Eloi" of the word on the cross?) does not seem especially prominent in Tobit or Haggai. Perhaps Orei inspired Micaiah rather than Micah (1 Kings 22. 8 ff.). And Astanfei possibly comes from *ashpath*, a word which means dunghill and is found in Ezra–Nehemiah.

Whatever the details may mean, the Ophite theory reflects an attempt to provide a rational justification for their source-criticism of the Old Testament.

Among the Valentinians there is a development in their analysis of the Law and the prophets. We possess two sharply contrasting statements, one from the oriental school (which seems to have been closer to Valentinus himself), the other from the western teacher Ptolemaeus. According to the orientals, "all the prophets and the Law spoke from the Demiurge, a foolish god, and they themselves were fools who knew nothing". This statement was justified by John 10. 4, "all who came before me were thieves and robbers", and Paul's reference to the mystery which was not known to previous generations.[1]

On the other hand, Ptolemaeus made a more careful, and more orthodox, analysis of the law in the Pentateuch.[2] It was derived partly from God, partly from Moses, and partly from the elders of the people. The part of the law which came from God was also tripartite. It consisted of pure legislation (the Decalogue), law mixed with injustice, and prefigurations, symbols, and images. At this point his doctrine was formally close to that of the apologist Justin, who also mentioned a threefold division of the law: ordained for piety and justice, for a mystery of Christ, and because of the people's hardheartedness.[3] But behind Ptolemaeus' triads, as Quispel has pointed out, lies the Valentinian mythology and anthropology.[4] Both eastern and western groups divided the teaching of Jesus into three parts. It was (1) figurative and mystical, (2) parabolic and enigmatical, and (3) clear and

---

[1] Hippolytus, *Ref.* 6. 35. 1.
[2] *Epistle to Flora*, in Epiphanius, *Pan. haer.* 33. 3–7.
[3] *Dial.* 44. 2.   [4] G. Quispel, *Ptolémée: Lettre à Flora* (Paris, 1949), Introduction.

evident.[1] The clear and evident part corresponds to the pure legislation in the Old Testament; the figurative and mystical, to the prefigurations, symbols, and images; and the parabolic and enigmatical, perhaps to the law mixed with injustice. As far as the Valentinians were concerned, what mattered was the clear and evident teaching. This, they said, was given the disciples only when Jesus was alone with them.[2] It was transmitted by secret tradition through Paul to a certain Theodas, and through Theodas to Valentinus himself.[3]

How then did the gospel come to be misunderstood by others? Irenaeus tells us how they explained this point.[4] The apostles hypocritically gave their teaching in accordance with the capacity of their hearers, and their answers in accordance with the presuppositions of those who asked questions. They made up "blind" stories for the blind in relation to their blindness, for the weak in relation to their weakness, for the mistaken in relation to their error. They proclaimed the Demiurge to those who thought he was the only God, but to those who had a conception of the unnameable Father, they expressed the ineffable mystery through parables and enigmas. Therefore the Lord and the apostles proclaimed the teaching not in accordance with the truth itself but hypocritically in relation to the capacity of each hearer.

In the above paragraph from Irenaeus there seems to be a certain inconsistency between the notion of hypocrisy and that of adaptation to the capacity of the audience. One might suspect that "hypocrisy" is Irenaeus' term to describe the method as envisaged by the Valentinians; their own idea would not necessarily go beyond adaptation to circumstances.

In any event, only Valentinians are capable of understanding the true teaching of Jesus, since the clear and evident portion of it was transmitted to them. In part the apostles perform the rôle of the elders of the people, who corrupted Old Testament teaching. But Valentinians are fortunate enough to possess the true teaching of the apostle Paul. Immediately after the passion he was sent to proclaim the resurrection. He was the equivalent of the Paraclete, who as Jesus said would teach all things (John 14. 26), would testify about Jesus (John 15. 26), and would glorify him (John 16. 14). Like the other

---

[1] Clement, *Excerpta ex Theodoto* 66.   [2] Cf. Mark 4. 34; John 16. 25.
[3] Clement, *Str.* 7. 106. 4.   [4] Irenaeus, *Adv. haer.* 3. 5. 1, p. 19 Harvey.

apostles, Paul preached in two ways. To those on the "left", inferior beings, he preached Jesus as having been born and having suffered; to those on the "right", he spoke of his birth from the Holy Spirit and the Virgin.[1] This notion is clearly based on Paul's statement that he cannot discuss spiritual truths with the Corinthians (1 Cor. 3. 1, 2; cf. 2. 6). It also reflects the absence of a doctrine of virginal conception from the Pauline epistles.

Irenaeus gives us a fairly systematic account of Valentinian exegesis.[2] The thirty heavenly aeons were to be found in the Saviour's age (Luke 3. 23), as well as in the total number of hours mentioned in the parable of the labourers in the vineyard (Matt. 20. 1–16: $3 + 6 + 9 + 11 + 1$). "These are great and ineffable mysteries", like the ineffable mystery of the apostles already mentioned. Moreover, Paul frequently refers to aeons, and in various parts of the gospels one can find the numbers 10, 12, and 18, important because the sum of the last two is thirty. Since Valentinian theology found its mythical centre in the fall of Sophia, the twelfth aeon, it discovered her experience intimated in Judas, the twelfth apostle, in the woman who had suffered for twelve years (Mark 5. 25), and in Jairus' daughter, who arose and walked, "for she was twelve years old" (Mark 5. 42). The peculiarity of Mark's expression would lead the exegete to suspect the presence of a hidden meaning. When Sophia fell outside the Pleroma, she was like an abortion. Paul hints at this fact in 1 Cor. 15. 8, where he compares himself to an abortion. She wore a veil to cover her shame, and Paul instructs women to wear such a veil in 1 Cor. 11. 10. Her suffering is also analogous to that of Jesus, and his cry, "My God, my God, why have you forsaken me?" was actually uttered by her as the Light left her. The universe came into existence out of her emotions, the equivalent of Jesus'. Her grief was his (Matt. 26. 38), like her fear (Matt. 26. 39) and her doubt (John 12. 27). And her further wanderings outside the Pleroma are really described in the parables of the lost sheep and the lost coin.

This is all exegesis of the prefigurative, mystical, parabolical, and enigmatical teaching of Jesus. Where are the clear and evident

[1] Clement, *Excerpta ex Theodoto* 23. 2, 3.
[2] *Adv. haer.* 1.1. 3; 1. 3. 1–4; 1. 8. 2–4; cf. F. M. Sagnard, *La gnose valentinienne* (Paris, 1947), 142.

examples? The Valentinians could have said that the Saviour and the apostle do mention Sophia (Luke 7. 35; 1 Cor. 2. 6). But presumably the only clear proofs were hidden in the secret tradition.

Finally Irenaeus reports exegetical proofs of the existence of the three classes of men. At this point the Valentinians could point to the fairly clear teaching of Paul in 1 Cor. 15. 48 and 2. 14, 15. To find the three classes in Jesus' words was more difficult. Fortunately Jesus seemed to have encountered three classes of inquirers in Luke 9. 58–61. To the men of matter and earth he said: "The Son of Man has no place (on earth) to lay his head." To psychics in need of rebirth he said: "No one who looks backward is ready for the kingdom of God." And to spirituals he said, setting them apart from the others: "Let the dead bury their dead." Similarly the three measures of meal (Luke 13. 21) refer to these groups.

When the Valentinians wanted to give further proofs for their doctrine of the heavenly Pleroma, they turned to the prologue to John. They were apparently the first interpreters to give detailed exegesis of it, exegesis reported by Irenaeus. The first verse, "In the beginning was the Logos, and the Logos was with God", meant that the Logos was located in the Beginning, or First Principle, and that this First Principle was in God. In the chain of coming-into-being, the Logos produced its partner (*syzygy*), Life; these two then produced Man and Church ("men" in John 1. 4). Logos, Life, Man, and Church made up the second Tetrad (group of four) among the aeons. What of the first Tetrad? This was revealed by the Saviour when he came, for he is called "Only-Begotten of the Father, full of Grace and Truth" (John 1. 14). These four, Only-Begotten, Father, Grace, and Truth, are the first Tetrad. "Thus John spoke about the first Ogdoad [four plus four], the Mother of all the aeons." Thus Valentinianism used the gospel of John for the names of the aeons. But in the gospel there is certainly no trace or aeons, tetrads, and an ogdoad. These were read into it by the Valentinians.

A little later in the second century, a Valentinian named Heracleon ventured to produce a collection of interpretations of the whole gospel, or at least of the first eight chapters. His comments are known to us because Origen used his work in his own *Commentary on John*. The fragments we possess are concerned with the prologue, with John the

Baptist as prophet and Echo of the Word, with Jesus' descent to Capernaum and ascent to Jerusalem and cleansing of the temple, with the Samaritan woman as Sophia and Christ as her partner, with the "royal officer" as the Creator-god, and with the relation of the devil to the three classes of men. Heracleon's exegesis is almost purely allegorical. Persons and places are understood as symbols of the three classes of men and of their heavenly counterparts. Thus Heracleon combines the Logos-Saviour with the spirituals and identifies both with the Holy of holies in the temple at Jerusalem. The Creator-god belongs with the psychics and is represented by John the Baptist and the "royal officer". The devil rules over men of matter and the material world, symbolized by Capernaum and Samaria. The Samaritan woman, Sophia, had committed fornication with matter and needed to be reunited with her partner, the Pleroma in the aeon. She is now the "spiritual church" through which Valentinians come to Jesus.

The point of departure for this exegesis is obviously the same as for other Valentinian interpretations. It is the Valentinian mythology and anthropology. At the same time, it may owe something to Marcion's treatment of Luke. For Marcion too, the "descent" of Jesus was not from one material place to another but from the spiritual world to this one. And for him John the Baptist was the servant of the Creator-god. Marcion had to alter the text of Luke to prove that Jesus' descent was from heaven. Heracleon uses the easier method of allegorization.

Valentinian exegesis obviously implies that the writings to be interpreted were inspired, though inspired to various degrees. And the Valentinians themselves were inspired, not so much in the work of exegesis as in the creation of their basic myths. Valentinus claimed that in a vision he saw an infant who said he was the Logos. This, says Hippolytus (*Ref.* 6. 42. 2), was the starting point of the whole Valentinian theology. In one of his Psalms, quoted by the same author (6. 37. 7), Valentinus explicitly spoke of various objects of his spiritual vision. Similarly, his disciple Marcus saw an inspired vision when the Tetrad appeared to him in female form (Irenaeus, *Adv. haer.* 1. 14. 1). The followers of Marcus shared his spiritual gift. They could prophesy when Marcus told them to do so. Though they might object that they had never prophesied before, they were instructed to say whatever came into their heads (ibid., 1. 13. 3). It seems likely that whatever they said could be allegorized by the master.

The Valentinians started out from their gnostic understanding of the meaning of human existence. Encountering the scriptures of the Church, they were impressed by many mysterious and apparently meaningless expressions which they alone could understand. And just as Philo had found God and the soul in the Old Testament, they proceeded to find the highest God, the Mother Sophia, and the three classes of men primarily in the gospels and the Pauline epistles. Like Philo, and like early Christian exegetes, they were inspired in their work of interpretation. In addition, they claimed that a secret tradition gave them the key to the hidden meaning of scriptures.

The Church, especially in the work of Irenaeus, gave its answer to gnostic allegorization by insisting on the common apostolic tradition, publicly acknowledged, in opposition to the secret gnostic tradition; by developing the apostolic symbol of faith which begins with the one God, creator of heaven and earth; by criticizing the gnostics' use of the allegorical method as proceeding from the obscure rather than from the obvious; and by insisting that the spiritual gift of exegesis was handed down in the public apostolic succession. The Church did not abandon the allegorical method, as we shall see, since it was necessary in dealing with obscure passages and other difficulties in scripture.

MONTANISM

Marcion and the other gnostics were not the only trouble-makers in second-century exegesis. Probably in the year 172 a certain Montanus, perhaps a convert from the worship of the Great Mother in Phrygia, came to the conviction that the last times were at hand and that the prophecies of the New Testament were to be fulfilled. He announced the arrival of the New Prophecy and the impending descent of the heavenly Jerusalem.

Prophecy had long been valued highly in the Church, as we know from the New Testament, the apostolic fathers, and the apologist Justin. But Montanus went beyond earlier prophets by claiming that God spoke directly through him and by blurring the distinction between God and his instrument. "I", said Montanus, "am the Father

F   73

and the Son and the Paraclete." His followers insisted that he was the Paraclete promised in John, as well as one of the prophets whose coming was foretold in Matt. 23. 24. Later writers state that they distinguished the Holy Spirit from the Paraclete, and held that only the Holy Spirit had been given the apostles (cf. John 20. 22). They argued that Paul himself predicted Montanus' coming, for he said, "We know in part, and we prophesy in part, but when that which is perfect comes, that which is imperfect will be abandoned" (1 Cor. 13. 9, 10). "That which is perfect" was obviously Montanus or his New Prophecy.

The Montanists claimed a kind of prophetic succession from apostolic times (Eusebius, *H.E.* 5. 17. 3, 4)—a succession running parallel not only to the apostolic succession of bishops but also to the secret succession of the gnostics. For their picture of the heavenly Jerusalem they relied on the Apocalypse of John, which had been envisioned "in the Spirit".

The Montanist movement created a crisis in the theory of inspiration. The Church had been content to speak of the inspiration of the Old Testament prophets. Now it was confronted with new prophets whose message differed from the gospel of the Church. Like Marcus' Tetrad, Christ appeared to the Montanist prophetess Priscilla in female form. The Church thus had to accept the New Prophecy or reject it and deny the inspiration of the Montanists. It chose the latter course, and attacked the Montanists in two ways. First, Christians argued that the Montanist prophets were excessively ecstatic. Since the distinction between excessive and ordinary ecstasy did not convey much meaning, the argument was sharpened. Ecstasy in any form is not characteristic of true prophecy. This argument is not strictly true, but in any event the passage of time first staled and then withered Montanism. Second, a certain Gaius of Rome denounced both the Gospel and the Apocalypse of John. He claimed that the Gospel disagreed with the synoptics (which it does), and that the Apocalypse was a forgery made in John's name by the Jewish-Christian heretic Cerinthus (which it is not). Later Christians soon rejected Gaius' arguments. He was trying to solve theological questions on the level of literary criticism. Such attempts have never been permanently successful, and his method may well have aroused painful memories of Marcion.

The Church thus answered Montanism by insisting that inspiration was limited to what came to be a canonical list of scripture, and by confining the working of the Spirit essentially to ministers of the apostolic succession.

In each of the three crises we have discussed, exegetical methodology played a secondary part. The theological problems were crucial. The basic point in every case was that the presuppositions of the Church were not those of the small sects which arose. But because everyone concerned believed in the importance of the written word of scripture, it was necessary for the Church to make more explicit what its own exegetical theory was. The working out of exegetical theory is to be found primarily in the works of three second-century churchmen. These writers are Justin of Rome (*c.* 150–65), Theophilus of Antioch (*c.* 180), and Irenaeus of Lyons (*c.* 180–5).

THE APOLOGISTS AND IRENAEUS

Justin was the first Christian writer we know who replied to Marcion. His work against him is lost, but from his *Apology* (about 150) and his later *Dialogue with Trypho* we can recover enough material to illustrate his methods of exegesis. We can see how he must have replied to Marcion. Indeed, scholars have sometimes suggested that his *Dialogue*, ostensibly a debate with a Jewish teacher, is really directed against Marcion's literal, "Jewish" exegesis of the Old Testament.

In both works Justin devotes many pages to proofs from prophecy which show that Jesus Christ is the Son of the God of the Old Testament. He claims that this kind of analysis will provide "the greatest and most truthful demonstration" of Christian doctrine. All the prophets were inspired by the Spirit or the Logos of God, and therefore all of them unanimously agree. How were they inspired? Justin tells us that at least two of them were in a state of ecstasy. These prophets were Daniel and Zechariah (*Dial.* 31. 7; 115. 3). And if these two prophesied ecstatically, obviously others, such as Isaiah and Ezekiel, did so under the same conditions.

It was natural for ecstatic prophets to speak mysteriously. They concealed the truth in parables and prefigurations; they spoke in enigmas and mysteries. Moreover, sometimes they simply predicted the future; sometimes they spoke as in the person of God, or of the people replying to God, or of Christ. For instance, Isaiah says: "The ox knows its owner and the ass the crib of its master, but Israel does not know me." It is really God who speaks, not Isaiah. Again, Psalm 22 is spoken partly in the person of Christ ("I stretched out my hands to an unbelieving and contradictory people"), partly in the person of the people ("Let him deliver himself"). Another difficulty is found in the prophets' description of the Christian future as if it were past. They seem to be speaking historically, while for Justin's purposes they must be predicting the future. And Jewish exegetes claimed that some of the prophecies had been fulfilled in Jewish history. Justin has to overcome all these difficulties in his effort to make the Old Testament Christian.

His basic claim is that the coming of Christ has made all the prophecies plain and clear. Moreover, the true understanding of the prophecies finally requires a gift of divine grace. This spiritual gift is found nowhere but among Christian interpreters.

Justin relies on the method of earlier Christians when he rejects Jewish exegesis of the Psalms. Thus David suffered none of the indignities mentioned in Ps. 22, while Jesus did. Therefore the Psalm refers to him. Jewish exegetes refer Ps. 24 and 110, as well as Isa. 7. 14, to King Hezekiah. But the "king of glory" in Ps. 24 can only be Jesus, who rose from the dead and ascended into heaven. Psalm 110. 4 speaks of an eternal priest of God; Hezekiah was not a priest. And the whole context of Isa. 7. 14 allegorically refers to Jesus, while it has no meaning in relation to Hezekiah. Justin uses the same Jewish-Christian method to argue that none of the Psalms refers to Solomon. This is the negative side of his exegesis.

On the positive side, he has to prove that the whole Old Testament is a prophecy of the coming of Jesus as the Messiah. He therefore makes use of a method much like that of Philo.[1] We cannot assume, however, that Justin had read Philo, since the method also reflects the exegetical rules of the rabbis.

1. Contradictions in scripture point to a hidden meaning. Thus God first tells Moses not to make images and then instructs him to make a brass serpent. The serpent must be a "mystery of Christ".

[1] C. Siegfried, *Philo von Alexandria als Ausleger des Alten Testaments* (Jena, 1875), 337–40.

2. Reduplicated expressions are significant. (Justin does not consider the possibility of faulty translation.[1]) Therefore we can find the "second God", the Logos, in Gen. 19. 24 ("the Lord rained . . . from the Lord"), Psalm 45 ("God, your God, anointed you"), and Psalm 110 ("the Lord said to my Lord").

3. Omissions are meaningful. Scripture does not say that Enoch, Noah, and others were circumcised, nor does it speak of promises given to Esau and Reuben.

4. Words have fixed allegorical meanings. If the day of the Lord is a thousand years in one passage, it is a thousand years elsewhere.

5. If words are ambiguous, they should be taken in such a way as to correspond with biblical teaching generally. Thus in Genesis God asks "where" someone is, not to get information but to convict of sin (3. 15 taken in the light of 4. 9).

6. Numbers, things, events, and names have symbolic meanings. Here Justin avoids Jewish and Marcionite literalism only to run the risk of falling into the trap set by Valentinians. And if questioned he could only have replied that the Old Testament was a prophecy of the coming of Christ and of the Christian Church. Only the Christian could understand the Old Testament. Other interpreters were unintelligent and wrongly regarded prophetic utterances as ambiguous (*Dial.* 36. 2; 51. 1, 2) !

While Justin treats the Old Testament as prophecy, he deals with the gospels in an entirely different way. (He never refers to the Pauline epistles, probably because he does not know what to make of Marcion's Paul.) Outsiders sometimes regard the gospel narrative as a (false) wonder-story; they classify it as poetry (*Apol.* 54. 2). Actually it is nothing of the sort. Jesus himself was no sophist or rhetorician; he used brief and compendious language (14. 5). The evangelists did not use rhetorical language but wrote *apomnemoneumata*, reminiscences of historical events. It is hard to tell where Justin got this idea of the gospels. It may be derived from Papias' mention of Mark's "remembering", or it may be Justin's own comparison with Xenophon's *Apomnemoneumata of Socrates*, a work he knows (*Apol.* 2. 11. 3).

Justin does not give exegesis of the gospels, probably because as historical works they need no exegesis. They speak for themselves.

---

[1] The Septuagint translation was not miraculous, however (*Apol.* 1. 30).

Of course, like the writings of Xenophon, they can contain allegories; but they were not written allegorically. Certain their authors were not ecstatically inspired. They were recording the fulfilment of prophecy.

Somewhere around Justin's time we find a similar understanding of prophecy and the gospel tradition in the pseudonymous 2 Peter. Its author insists on the inspired character of prophecy. "Prophecy was never controlled by human volition; men inspired by the Holy Spirit spoke from God" (1. 21). The author is perhaps attacking Montanist or Valentinian prophets who could apparently decide when they should go into a trance. And he insists that "no prophecy of scripture is to be given individual exegesis". This may mean that scripture is to be considered as a whole; more probably, it means that there is an exegetical tradition which is binding on individual exegetes. The latter interpretation seems to be confirmed by another passage (3. 16), in which the author condemns the forced exegesis of those who "torture" obscure passages in the Pauline epistles, as well as the other scriptures. By the time and in the place he writes, the Pauline epistles are clearly on the same level as the Old Testament. The "torture" could be either Marcionite or Valentinian exegesis.

His treatment of the gospel tradition is like Justin's. He insists that the gospels do not contain the kind of myths used by sophists but are the product of eye-witnesses (1. 16). They were written so that later Christians might always remember these things, even after the apostolic age (1. 15).

Thus 2 Peter and Justin agree in insisting that the Old Testament can be understood only by Christians, and /that the gospels are historical documents. The gospels are not allegories and cannot be allegorized.

A generation later, an even fuller analysis of prophetic inspiration is provided by Theophilus, Bishop of Antioch. His treatise against Marcion is now lost, but we may suspect that it did not greatly differ in its view of prophecy from what we have in his books *To Autolycus*.

According to Theophilus, the holy scriptures were written by holy prophets, who "through the Spirit of God ¹predicted the past in the way in which it took place, the present in the way in which it is taking place, and the future in the order in which events will be accomplished" (1. 14). These prophets, inspired by God or his Logos or his Wisdom or his Spirit, became "instruments of God" and spoke in harmony (2. 9, 10).

They were obviously inspired in describing the past, for on the one hand they were not present at the creation (2. 10) and on the other hand the surpassing greatness and richness of God's work makes inspiration necessary in writing an account worthy of the work (2. 12).

Theophilus' allusion to the "surpassing greatness and richness" sounds almost like an allusion to Marcion's *Antitheses*, with its stress on the wonderful nature of revelation. Perhaps he is hinting that if the gospel is so inspired, the prophets must have enjoyed the same gift of revelation. More certainly, he is attacking the idea that the inspiration of Homer and Hesiod can be compared with that of the prophets. No man, he says, could say anything worthy of the work of creation, even if he had ten thousand tongues. This is an allusion to Homer's own invocation of the Muses. And Theophilus goes on to attack Hesiod explicitly. Poets like Hesiod claimed divine inspiration from the Muses for their description of the origin of the universe. This claim is ridiculous. The Muses knew nothing about creation, for they came into existence later. The poets were actually led astray by their own imaginations. The spirit that led them was not a pure spirit but one of error (2. 8).

At the same time, Theophilus does not limit inspiration to the Old Testament. He refers to the Sibyl as "a prophetess among the Greeks and the other nations" (2. 36). And he speaks of "the holy scriptures and all the inspired men" (2. 22), one of whom is the evangelist John. Phrases from the Pauline epistles are ascribed to "the divine Logos" (3. 14). And in order to understand even the chronology of the Old Testament the exegete needs God's gift of truth and grace (3. 23). Probably, therefore, only the Spirit-guided interpreter can understand the true meaning of the Old Testament, the gospels and epistles, and the Sibyl's prophecies.

Such an exegete can recognize that the story of creation is not simply history. Written by the inspired Moses, it contains "signs" and "prefigurations". For example, the luminaries themselves contain a sign and prefiguration of "a great mystery". The sun is a prefiguration of God, the moon of man (waxing and waning). The three days before the creation of the luminaries prefigure the triad God-Logos-Sophia. The stars too contain "a disposition and arrangement". The brightest ones are "in imitation of the prophets"; the less brilliant ones are prefigurations of "the people of the righteous"; and the wandering planets are prefigurations of those men who depart from God (2. 15). Moreover, marine monsters and carnivorous birds are "in the likeness of covetous men and transgressors" (2. 16), while quadrupeds and wild animals are prefigurations of certain men who neither know nor honour God (2. 17).

In all these instances of cosmic symbolism, there is no difference between "prefiguration" (*typos*) and "sign" (*deigma*), or between both these words and "likeness" or "imitation". Theophilus means only that these created objects are examples which prefigure God and man. His exegesis is close to rabbinic interpretations of Genesis.

He notes that "it is written mysteriously in Genesis that man was placed twice in Paradise" (2. 26). The first narrative was "fulfilled" when he was actually placed there; the second is going to be fulfilled after the resurrection and judgement. Here again Theophilus does not go beyond rabbinic interpreters. We might expect some mention of Christ as the Second Adam, but we find none. In his analysis of the work of the first Adam (2. 24–7) he often uses language which recalls New Testament teaching about Christ, but his meaning is never made explicit. Either as an apologist or as an anti-Marcionite writer, he cannot (or at any rate, does not) find Christ in the Old Testament as freely as Justin found him.

Theophilus is close to Judaism. He values the law very highly. It was given by the prophet Moses, and the later prophets were sent to remind the people of the law (3. 11), just as the Johannine Paraclete was sent to remind Christians of Jesus' teaching (John 14. 26). The law is essentially the Decalogue. But Theophilus lists ten commandments from which the third (blasphemy) and fourth (Sabbath) are omitted, while some "judgements" from Ex. 23 are added. Apparently he is correcting the law in terms of the gospel; he undoubtedly knows that Jesus was accused of blasphemy and of Sabbath-breaking.[1]

[1] Theophilus is also close to the Jewish-Christian theory of interpolations, set forth in the *Clementine Homilies* and *Recognitions*. The Ebionites believed that Jesus came to set forth what was true and what was false in the Old Testament; he pointed out the

Hère we find an example of the wide variety present within orthodox exegesis in the second century. Theophilus' interpretation is much more restrained, more literal (generally speaking) than Justin's. There is an emphasis on history which later comes to the fore in the exegetical school of Antioch. And by implication this emphasis on history involves rejecting the unhistorical literalism of Marcion or the unhistorical allegorizations of the gnostics. The prophets were inspired not only as predicters but as historians. The evangelists too were inspired.

Finally, in the work of Irenaeus of Lyons *Against Heresies* we find an explicit refutation of the errors of Valentinian and Marcionite exegesis. Like Theophilus, Irenaeus insisted on the inspiration of the apostles as well as that of the prophets. The whole Bible is spiritual (2. 28. 3). The same Spirit spoke through the prophets, the apostles, and the elders of the apostolic Church (3. 21. 3).

Irenaeus is the first Christian writer to introduce an apocalyptic legend which makes the inspiration of the Old Testament thoroughly miraculous. This legend, found in 2 Esdras (14. 21–47), tells us that at the time of the Exile the law was burned. The scribe Ezra prayed for the gift of God's Spirit so that he could reproduce the biblical history and the law. After a vision, he and five equally inspired assistants spent forty days in rewriting not only the twenty-four books of the Old Testament, but also seventy apocryphal writings.

Irenaeus accepts this legend and uses it in an *a fortiori* argument to show that the Greek translation of the Old Testament was clearly made "by the inspiration of God" (3. 21. 2). He wants to safeguard the Septuagint version against Jewish or Jewish-Christian translators who substitute "young woman" for "virgin" in Isa. 7. 14.

At the same time, he does not speak of ecstasy when he discusses prophetic inspiration, and he recognizes the human element in inspiration

---

interpolations, which dealt with sacrifices, the temple cultus, and the kingship, and contained prophecies not related to the messianic age, and theological statements unworthy of God. He transmitted this "mystery of the scriptures" to Peter, who in turn delivered it to the Ebionites (cf. H. J. Schoeps, *Theologie und Geschichte des Judenchristentums*, Tübingen, 1949, 150—3; *Urgemeinde—Judenchristentum—Gnosis*, Tübingen, 1956, 26–9). According to Schoeps this theory is specifically directed against Marcion; but of course it was anticipated by Posidonius and, as we have tried to show, by Paul.

as earlier writers had not recognized it. Thus in criticizing gnostic allegorization of the Pauline epistles, he says (3. 7. 2) that

> the apostle frequently transposes the order of words (*a*) on account of the rapidity of his discourses and (*b*) on account of the impetus of the Spirit which is in him.

Irenaeus by no means neglects the inspiration of Paul. He only wishes to show that the peculiar order of his words does not contain a hidden meaning. Elsewhere he says that the apostles were filled with the power of the Holy Spirit from on high and possessed "perfect knowledge". This perfect knowledge was handed down in the four gospels, which contain the written teaching of the apostles Matthew, Peter, Paul, and John (3. 1. 1, 2).

Irenaeus rejects the gnostic (and earlier orthodox) view that the gospel was transmitted not in writing but through the "living voice" (3. 2. 1). The fourfold written gospel is the "pillar and ground of the Church" (3. 11. 8). And since he holds that the Septuagint translators were inspired, he must believe that there is an inspired translation of Matthew, since it was written in Hebrew (3. 1. 1). He does not refer to Papias' picture of a number of translators.

With the Valentinians Irenaeus feels the need of an authoritative exegetical tradition. Unlike them, he finds it in the common apostolic tradition and succession, not secret but open and known to all. With the apostolic elders is the apostolic doctrine (4. 32. 1). Something remains, however, for the individual exegete who stands within the Church. He needs rational rules to guide his work, not Valentinian "divination" (1. 9. 1). Therefore Irenaeus insists that the plain and unambiguous passages of scripture must serve as the guide for dealing with such dark passages as the parables (2. 27. 1). The gnostics pay no attention to context, and for this reason their exegesis can be compared to taking a mosaic of a king and rearranging it into a picture of a dog (1. 8. 1).

The ultimate standard, however, is the apostolic rule of faith. And while Irenaeus criticizes gnostics for allegorizing in contradiction to it, he does not hesitate to use the same method. He holds that the Mosaic law consisted of prefigurations, except where it was setting forth the law of nature, as in the Decalogue (4. 14. 3). It was given to lead the people "through the secondary to the primary, through the temporal to the eternal, through the carnal to the spiritual, through the earthly to the heavenly". When Moses was on the mount, "for forty days he learned to comprehend the *logoi* of God and the heavenly forms and the spiritual images and the prefigurings of future things". Here Irenaeus reproduces the Philonic-Platonic doctrine of heavenly patterns as expressed in Hebrews.

At the same time, he holds that nothing in the Old Testament is without a hidden meaning. It is understood only in the light of Christ's coming, for "every prophecy is an enigma and a contradiction to men before its fulfilment" (4. 26. 1). This is why the stories in the law seem like mythology to the Jews when they read them. Christians can explain the lives of the patriarchs by seeking the prefiguration of Jesus in them (4. 20–2).

Irenaeus was not content to treat Old Testament figures as prefigurations of Christ. He worked out a positive theology of history on the basis of his exegesis. It goes back in essence to the apostle Paul, but it is much more systematically developed. We find it in the fourth book of his treatise.

His doctrine of universal salvation through the Logos allows him to maintain the view that before the coming of the law there was a natural law by which some men lived. This natural law, which remains permanently necessary as the foundation of morality, is expressed in the Decalogue. However, during their slavery in Egypt the fathers sinned; justice and the love of God came to an end. The law of Moses was therefore historically necessary in order to bring the people back to God. The "letters of Moses" are also words of Christ; they have two meanings, one figurative and the other the true meaning signified in the figure. The people had to learn to fear God by taking the figures literally. They had to pass through slavery before they were ready for freedom. And the special legislation of the Jews was given "for the hardness of their hearts", just as similar legislation was given by Paul in 1 Corinthians. The first covenant, then, was given men in order to enslave men to God for their own benefit. It could not have been for God's benefit, since he does not need service. And it also showed them prefigurations of heavenly things; they were not yet ready to see the realities.

The tragedy of Jewish exegetes lies in their failure to accept the incarnate Logos. They think that by themselves they are able to know God. They are led to contradict the law, as when they prohibit healings on the Sabbath. Jesus argued against them; he said that they repeated the words of the law but lacked love and therefore were unjust towards God and neighbour. The special legislation came to an end with John the Baptist. Indeed, the prophets had already predicted the end of the cultus and the literal law, as well as the coming of Christ. Christ, however, did not actually contradict the law (as Marcion supposed). He extended the law and "filled it full", especially the Decalogue. His work of fulfilment is to be found especially in his counsels of perfection, which extend the range of the Decalogue beyond actions to desires. He did not annul it, since it is to be found in both Testaments. In his coming men were given the power to abstain from evil works and the desire for them.

This is the Church's systematic answer to Marcion, Valentinus, and (by implication) Montanus. The Church does not deny the inspiration of the Old Testament but extends it to the New. It does not reject the allegorical method but insists that the starting-point must be the Church's faith. It does not repudiate tradition as a guide for exegesis but holds that the tradition must be the open, legitimate apostolic tradition.

Above all, the Church appeals to history. Marcion tried to separate Christianity from ʾhistory, especially the Old Testament history. Valentinus tried to cut it off from the world. Montanus tried to concentrate on prophecy rather than on the saving events of the past. The answer of Irenaeus to all three is an insistence on the centrality of the apostolic witness to Christ. He develops a theology of history in answer to the unhistorical exegesis of his predecessors. And like his later follower Tertullian, he insists on the authoritative nature of this theology. The appeal to history means an appeal to tradition. To a considerable extent, the allegorization at Alexandria is a reaction from this concentration on historical reality, and the authority of past events. There the study of Philo is fused with gnostic and Christian insights to create a new allegorization.

5

ALEXANDRIAN ALLEGORISTS

WE have now seen that at the end of the second century the Church had firmly rejected the unhistorical literary criticism, allegorization, and "prophetization" of Marcion, Valentinus, and Montanus. The Bible was the Church's book, and the Church had come to general agreement that the book was the inspired record of an historical revelation. While there was still room for exegetical freedom, this freedom was severely limited by the insistence on history and, to a considerable extent, on literal interpretation.

In one Church, however, the allegorical method continued to flourish. This was the Church of Alexandria, in which prominent gnostics had apparently taught during the second century and several apocryphal gospels had been produced. Towards the end of the century a catechetical school was founded by a certain Pantaenus, but he is little more than a name. The first great Christian teacher of Alexandria was Clement, who became head of the school about the year 200.

CLEMENT

Clement lays little stress on the inspiration of scripture. He usually takes it for granted, though at one point he speaks of the prophets as instruments of the divine voice (*Str.* 6. 168. 3). Elsewhere he argues in favour of this inspiration by comparing it with that of the poets as discussed by Plato (*Ion*) and Democritus. He also compares the voice of God at Sinai with Greek oracular utterance (*Str.* 6. 33. 3).[1] The form of inspiration may be the same for Hebrews and for Greeks. But the source of inspiration is quite different. Seers predicted the future partly on the basis of observation and probabilities, partly under demonic influence; the prophets and the Sibyl were moved by the power and inspiration of God (*Str.* 1. 135. 2, 3). At this point Clement apparently follows Theophilus. From Irenaeus he adds that Ezra and the Greek translators were also inspired.[2] The stage has thus been

---

[1] R. M. Grant, *Miracle and Natural Law in Graeco-Roman and Early Christian Thought* (Amsterdam, 1952), 197.   [2] *Str.* 1. 149. 3.

set for a thorough-going allegorization of scripture, which Clement is not slow to provide. In producing it he makes frequent use of the works of Philo, but unlike Philo he feels the need for a rational defence of the allegorical method. This is given in the fifth book of his *Stromateis*.[1]

His long account of the universality of symbolism is probably based on either one or two Neopythagorean documents;[2] and in it he states that "all theologians, barbarian and Greek, hid the beginnings of things and delivered the truth in enigmas and symbols,[3] allegories and metaphors and similar figures".[4] The barbarians are first of all the Egyptians, who used hieroglyphic writing; the Greeks include deliverers of oracles, wise men, and poets "who philosophized many things through allegory"—Orpheus, Linus, Musaeus, Homer, Hesiod, and the wise men.[5] Thus his point of view is essentially the same as that of Plutarch, Numenius, and Celsus. Like Numenius, whom he mentions,[6] he holds that Plato is a Greek-speaking Moses.

On this ground he can hold that the enigmatic method of speech was derived from the prophets, for the Spirit says through Isaiah (45. 3), "I will give you treasures, hidden, dark", and in Psalm 78. 2, "I will open my mouth in parables". The apostle Paul confirms the use of this method in 1 Cor. 2. 6–8 and elsewhere.[7]

Clement then proceeds to discuss Pythagoras' use of symbols to convey a teaching derived from Moses; then he gives some examples of poetic allegory; finally he comes back to the Old Testament. Following Philo he states that almost the whole of scripture is expressed in enigmas.[8] An example is the symbolic meaning of the tabernacle in Jerusalem.

We now start over again, thus perhaps making use of a second source document. The Egyptians "did not divulge the knowledge of divine things to the profane". There are symbols in hieroglyphic writing, among barbarian kings, in "Ephesian letters", and in symbolic circles. Furthermore, the grammarian Didymus of Alexandria has

---

[1] *Str.* 5. 20. 3—82. 4.

[2] Ibid., 5. 20. 3—31. 5; 41–50; cf. W. Bousset, *Jüdisch-christlicher Schulbetrieb in Alexandria und Rom* (Göttingen, 1915), 235; J. Munck, *Untersuchungen über Klemens von Alexandria* (Stuttgart, 1933), 131.

[3] The words of Cornutus.   [4] *Str.* 5. 21. 4.   [5] Ibid., 5. 24. 1.

[6] Ibid., 1. 150. 4.   [7] Ibid., 5. 23. 2—26. 5.   [8] Ibid., 5. 32. 1.

said that "the use of symbolical speech is characteristic of the wise man, as is the explanation of what is meant by it".[1] More examples follow, from Greek and barbarian religion, from Orphism and Pythagoreanism, and (once more) from the Old Testament. This time the allegorical meaning of the Old Testament is proved not only from Paul but also from Barnabas.[2]

This analysis rests upon the idea of a universal revelation by the Logos. In another passage[3] Clement traces successions of teachers from Greek philosophers back to Pythagoras, Pherecydes, Thales, and the first wise men. Farther back are the Egyptians, Indians, Babylonians, and Magi. Finally we get back to the first generation of men, inspired by the Logos. Alternatively he can hold that poets, philosophers, and wise men stole their ideas from the Old Testament. This notion means that for one barbarian origin of Greek culture Clement substitutes another. The Old Testament becomes, as among Hellenistic Jews, the primitive source of what is true in the Greek theological tradition.

But with all these proofs that symbolic language is often used, Clement has still not clearly shown why it is used; he finally supplies two reasons. The first is that divine mysteries should not be revealed to the profane (a point already intimated by the Egyptians). This point can be proved from Greek philosophers, Paul, Barnabas, the prophets, and Plato. For in his *Second Epistle* (312 d) Plato said, "We must speak to you (of God) in enigmas". This idea is expressed by Paul in 1 Cor. 2. 6, 7. The highest authority is thus the combination of philosophy and Christianity. Clement is upheld in his view that divine mysteries are only for believers.

The second reason is that in any case teaching about God can be only symbolical, since Plato, Moses, and Paul agree that "to find him is difficult, and to declare him to all is impossible". This sentence of Plato (*Timaeus* 28 c) had been a favourite of Middle Platonists and Christian apologists. Clement extends its meaning to cover the allegorical method.

---

[1] *Str.* 5. 46. 2.
[2] Ibid., 5. 63; but Barnabas is not an absolutely reliable authority for Clement; cf. R. M. Grant, *Miracle and Natural Law in Graeco-Roman and Early Christian Thought* (Amsterdam, 1952), 197.
[3] Ibid., 6. 57. 3; cf. E. Molland in *Symbolae Osloenses* 15–16 (1936), 64.

This is all that he says on the subject in his fifth book. To the two reasons already mentioned he adds a third when he considers the subject again in his sixth book (*Str.* 6. 126–32). The allegorical sense is hidden so that intelligent men may become inquisitive about it. The holy mysteries are veiled in parables, and a parable is "a narrative based on some subject not the principal subject, similar to the principal subject and leading him who understands to the true and principal matter". Clement takes such a definition from Greek grammar. As usual, he adds examples, this time from the teaching of Christ and the apocryphal *Preaching of Peter*. His best proof comes from Prov. 1. 5, 6:

> He who hears these prophets, being wise, will be wiser. And the intelligent man will acquire rule, and will understand a parable and a dark saying, the words and enigmas of the wise.

Not so satisfactory is an allegorical explanation of the *Shepherd* of Hermas. Hermas transcribed the book given him by the Church. He copied the letters but only later understood the syllables. So the allegorizer learns to go beyond the letter.

For three reasons, then, says Clement, these allegories are to be found in scripture. The true doctrine is hidden from the profane; in any case, God can be spoken of only in symbolic language; and for the "true gnostic" (Clement's ideal Christian) the symbols arouse curiosity. It is obvious that any of the second-century gnostics could have said the same. It is worth noting that Clement never criticized them for allegorizing scripture, presumably because his own view was so much like theirs. He agreed with the gnostic Isidore, son of Basilides, that the ancient poet Pherecydes spoke allegorically (*Str.* 6. 53. 5; 5. 50. 3).[1]

Given the existence of these allegories, how was Clement to extract their real meaning? R. P. C. Hanson has shown convincingly that Clement believed in a secret tradition which included the allegorical method.[2] This "gnosis" was given by Christ after the resurrection to three apostles. They transmitted it to the others, and the others to the Seventy—of whom Barnabas was one. Clement, as we have seen,

---

[1] The Antitactae are wrong because they take scriptural allegories literally (*Str.* 3. 38. 1); Stoic allegorizers are wrong because they have no true tradition (*Str.* 5. 89. 2).

[2] *Origen's Doctrine of Tradition* (London, 1954), 67–9.

uses Barnabas as one of his witnesses for the allegorical method, a method which Barnabas calls "gnosis".

Thus we see that Clement goes beyond simple allegorization to the truly gnostic idea of secret tradition. The post-resurrection revelation through three apostles to all is almost exactly what we have in the newly discovered Valentinian *Letter of James*. Mondésert has spoken of Clement's "esoteric attitude",[1] but it is more than that. As far as exegesis is concerned, Clement is very close to Valentinian gnosticism, though his results are quite different from theirs.

Perhaps what Clement has done is to come as close to gnosis as he can, using gnostic terminology in order to lead gnostics to Christian theology. At times he lets his terminology get the better of his ideas. Such a result is facilitated by what W. den Boer has called his "associative thought form".[2] In any event, Clement has not provided any systematic philosophical or theological justification for Christian allegorization. His secret tradition can be matched by gnostic exegetes, as we have seen, and when he gives a lengthy exposition of his own "gnostic interpretation",[3] we find that it largely based on Aristobulus and Philo.[4] Indeed, his analysis of the Mosaic legislation as historical, legislative, ceremonial (related to physics), and theological is simply a revision of what Philo had said.[5]

Moreover, apart from occasional bits of symbolic exegesis, Clement allegorizes only the Old Testament, presumably because on the one hand he had Philonic precedent for this effort and on the other he was afraid of the allegorizations made by the Valentinians and others. He does not treat the New Testament and the story of Jesus allegorically.

This is the most important advance over Clement's work which we find in the exegesis of Origen. Origen not only treats the gospels allegorically but also provides a careful and detailed explanation of why he does so.

---

[1] C. Mondésert, *Clément d'Alexandria* (Paris, 1944), 61.
[2] *De allegorese in het werk van Clemens Alexandrinus* (Leiden, 1940), 1–14.
[3] *Str.* 6. 133–48.
[4] Mondésert (op. cit., 172–81) has carefully shown the extent of Philo's influence on Clement in *Str.* 5. 32–40.
[5] *Str.* 1. 176. 1, 2; on the text, E. Peterson in *Theologische Literaturzeitung* 56 (1931), 69–70; on the relation to Philo, H. Wolfson, *The Philosophy of the Church Fathers* I (Cambridge, 1956), 52–5.

ORIGEN

Before we can turn to Origen's systematic treatment of allegorization in his treatise *On First Principles* and his practical demonstration of principles in the *Commentary on John*, we must consider his earlier exegetical essays in order to see how his thought developed. He was master of the catechetical school at Alexandria from 204 to 232, when he left for Caesarea after a bitter conflict with the bishop, Demetrius. At Alexandria, according to Eusebius of Caesarea (*H.E.* 6. 24), he wrote the first five books of his *Commentary on John*, the first eight books of his *Commentary on Genesis*, a *Commentary on Psalms* 1–25, a *Commentary on Lamentations*, a treatise *On the Resurrection*, a treatise *On First Principles*, and ten books of *Stromateis* ("Miscellanies" like Clement's).

This list is not arranged chronologically, and the sequence of Origen's early works has been established only by modern scholars.[1] It is approximately as follows:

> *On the Resurrection, Stromateis, Commentary on Psalms*
> *Commentary on Lamentations*
> *Commentary on Genesis* (first three books)
> *On First Principles*
> *Commentary on Genesis* (last five books)
> *Commentary on John* (first five books)

Since the treatise *On the Resurrection* and the *Stromateis* were not specifically exegetical works, Origen dealt with exegesis only in producing proofs for his views. Paul's epistles naturally provided materials for his doctrine of resurrection (Lomm. 17. 63, 64). And in various books of the *Stromateis* we find exegesis of passages from both testaments. Origen's basic attitude is expressed in a fragment (Lomm. 17. 75) in which he is explaining Christian freedom on the basis of Gal. 5. 13: "He who is free, and follows spirit and truth in the higher sense, despises both the older prefigurations and the letter; but he should not despise the lesser persons." Condemning literalism does not involve condemning literalists. But Origen was absolutely convinced that Paul was an allegorist; he adduced 1 Cor. 10. 9 as proof of his point.[2]

[1] R. Cadiou, *La jeunesse d'Origène* (Paris, 1935); cf. Hanson, op. cit., 1–30.

[2] E. von der Goltz, *Eine textkritische Arbeit des zehnten bezw. sechsten Jahrhunderts* (*Texte und Untersuchungen* 17, 4, Leipzig, 1899), 66.

His earliest commentary was probably that on Psalms 1–25, perhaps stimulated by a similar work of Hippolytus.[1] In his preface Origen speaks of the mysterious character of scripture, which is full of enigmas, parables, and dark sayings. In fact, as the Bible itself says, it is locked and sealed (cf. Ex. 28. 36; Rev. 3. 7, 8). In order to interpret it the exegete therefore needs divine aid. Origen agrees with a Hebrew teacher who said of the Old Testament, "Because of the lack of clarity in it, it is like many locked rooms in one house, each with a different key". The exegete, as Paul shows (1 Cor. 2. 13), must find the right keys and fit them to the locks. This task is important because the scriptures are completely and verbally inspired.

Origen then proceeds to speak of the titles of the Psalms, explaining them allegorically, and turns to a fairly conventional exegesis of each one. He agrees at most points with the traditional exegesis of Psalm 3, as Guillet has shown.[2] The only striking points are his extended attack on a doctrine of physical resurrection (on Psalm 1. 5) and his reference to "the laws of *anagogé*", a phrase he uses to replace Philo's "laws of allegory" (Lomm. 11. 425). *Anagogé* is a word which points more towards the inner meaning of scripture than to its literary form.

His next commentary, that on Lamentations, may have been written after a visit to Jerusalem, but we cannot be certain. The preface deals with the descent of the soul in Philonic terms, and in the body of the commentary this descent is taken to be the central theme of the biblical book. Jerusalem means the soul. This commentary is more carefully developed than the one on the Psalms, for Origen is trying to find one theme running through the allegories of his inspired author. He follows the method used by Philo in his *Questions and Answers on Genesis and Exodus*. First he discusses the literal meaning of a text; then he gives the inner meaning (*dianoia*) in accordance with "the laws of *anagogé*" (Klost. 245. 23). The verb "allegorize" occurs only once.(248. 8). What Origen is trying to do is to make use of Philo's method for a Philonic purpose. Apparently, however, he already feels uneasy about Philo's terminology.

After writing on Lamentations, Origen turned to a far more

[1] Cadiou, op. cit., 89.
[2] J. Guillet in *Rech. de sc. rel.* 34 (1947), 261–71.

demanding exegetical endeavour. This was the creation of his *Commentary on Genesis*, a biblical book in which were to be found most of the themes of his gradually developing philosophical theology. Genesis, moreover, had been used by heretical theologians who had taken some of its expressions literally. One of these theologians was Hermogenes, whose views Origen had already criticized in interpreting Psalm 19 (Lomm. 12. 73). And in the *Commentary on Genesis* he is arguing against someone like Hermogenes when he states that God never began to be a Father, but was always Father (Lomm. 8. 4) and denounces exegetes who refer Gen. 1. 2 to pre-existent matter (5, 6). Origen implicitly claims to be defending the true tradition of the Church.

He began his commentary by stressing, once more, the necessity of "spiritual understanding" along with the exegete's recognition of his own limitations (Lomm. 8. 1–3). Unfortunately we do not possess all of this commentary, and it is not entirely clear why Origen broke off his writing of it before he reached Gen. 1. 26.[1] Probably because of criticisms, he stopped and turned to the preparation of a major theological work in which he could justify both his theology and his exegetical method.

He was doubtless aware of the scandal which might result from his exegesis of later passages in Genesis, and thought that he ought to justify such statements as his comments on the garden of Eden. "When in reading we ascend from myths and from literal interpretation, we inquire what trees those were which God put in his garden; we say that there was in that place not one tree perceptible by the senses."[2] Eden was not a place. Its name was related to the Greek word *hedy*, sweet, and the garden was really the Church.[3] The coats of skin (Gen. 3. 21) which Adam and Eve acquired were human bodies.[4] In order to set forth such doctrines as these, Origen had to declare his loyalty to the Church's tradition and define the task of the exegete.

He therefore begins his treatise *On First Principles* by declaring that the sole norm of belief is "the ecclesiastical and apostolic tradition". This tradition involves belief in the one God, the Creator; in

---

[1] That he did so is plain from *Princ.* 1. 2. 6.
[2] Lommatzsch 8. 55, 56.   [3] Ibid., 56, 57.   [4] Ibid., 58.

Christ Jesus and his incarnation, death, resurrection, and ascension; in the Holy Spirit, the soul, and the resurrection of the dead.[1] But while the apostles delivered these fundamental doctrines openly to all, they left rational arguments and questions about "how" and "whence" to the "lovers of wisdom". Origen's statement means that for him the apostles have the rôle of "the most ancient theologians and poets" who according to Plutarch dealt with final and efficient causes; he himself, like the "physicists", is to be concerned with formal and material causes.[2] The Christian philosopher can therefore discuss the origin of the soul, the devil, and angels; the animate character of sun, moon, and stars; and the circumstances before creation and after the end of the world.

He does not confine himself to these matters, however. From the Church's tradition we learn that "the scriptures were written through the Spirit of God, and they possess not only the obvious meaning but also another which is hidden from most people; for the things which are written are likenesses of certain mysteries and images of divine matters". The whole Church, he says, agrees in believing that the whole law is "spiritual" (Rom. 7. 14). It also admits that the intimations of the law are known not to all, but to those to whom the grace of the Holy Spirit is given (cf. 1 Cor. 12. 8).

The meaning of Origen's affirmation of faith becomes clear when he later describes the essential content of the spiritual meaning (*Princ.* 4. 2. 7, 8). This is the true "scope" or reference of scripture. To understand it is to understand how scripture really speaks of God and his Son, the Son's nature, the mode and causes of the incarnation, the Son's activity, and the nature of the persons and occasions involved in revelation. It is to understand the fall of the angels, the differences among souls, and other theological problems. The spiritual understanding of scripture is therefore the means for comprehending not only the basic tradition but also the other matters reserved for "lovers of wisdom". In short, all Christian doctrine ultimately rests on allegorization. The Christian who best understands scripture is the one who realizes that the Holy Spirit used the guise of historical writing only as a means for teaching philosophical theology (4. 2. 8).

---

[1] Cf. J. N. D. Kelly, *Early Christian Creeds* (London, 1950), 92, 93.
[2] *De defectu* 47, 48; see above, Chapter 1, p. 14.

Origen had already insisted on philosophical theology in his earlier works. In commenting on the first Psalm he had said that the lover of truth must try "to preserve the tradition of the ancients and at the same time avoid falling into the nonsense of impoverished notions which are at once impossible and unworthy of God".[1] Now in this treatise he explained what "impoverished notions" were. They resulted from literalism and led to three kinds of errors. (1) The Jews took scripture as related to sense-perception and therefore failed to understand the prophecies of Christ. (2) The heretics ascribed anthropomorphic expressions to the Creator-god and used myths as the foundation of their own theology. (3) Simple believers do not understand Origen's theology. They admit that there are mystical references to God's plan of salvation, but they have no real conception of what God's plan is.

Obviously Origen's real target is the simple believer, and he is the target not because he rejects the allegorical method (he often accepts it), but because he does not accept Origen's explanation of what the allegory means. Origen adds that the simple believer must realize that a gift of grace is needed for understanding the "mind" of the gospels as well as of the Old Testament. The Apocalypse contains hidden mysteries. And while some may suppose that the Pauline epistles are plain and clear, actually they are full of great thoughts which require exegesis.

He now proceeds to argue that there is a triple sense in scripture, corresponding to a triple division of human nature. Scripture, like man, consists of flesh, soul, and spirit. Its flesh is the literal meaning, which the simple believer can understand. Its soul is understood by the less simple. Its spirit is made known to the believer who is truly spiritual.

Scholars have often noted that in Origen's later works this triple division fades away. It actually breaks down immediately. Origen tries to prove his case by allegorizing the *Shepherd* of Hermas. Hermas was told to send his revelation to Grapté and to Clement, "who deals with those outside". Grapté is the literal, written (*grapton*) meaning of scripture, while Clement deals with those who are outside inferior, bodily thoughts. There are thus two senses, not three. In so far as

[1] Epiphanius, *Pan. haer.* 64. 14. 1.

there is any real difference between the soul and the spirit of scripture, it corresponds roughly to the difference between what the Stoics and Philo called "physical" (theological) allegory and what they called "ethical".

Origin still has not adequately answered the question which troubled Clement. Why should there be allegories in scripture? Why was the meaning not set forth simply and clearly? The answer he gives is based on the nature of the universe and of God's working in the universe. In discussing creation he has already argued that Nature itself is an allegory, concealing the hidden operations of providence. Without the "stumbling-blocks" in Nature men might neglect the operation of God; they might not turn from the creation to the Creator. So in scripture there are grounds of offence and impossibilities which force the reader to look farther.[1] Spiritual believers will understand; simple believers cannot understand anyway. In other words, it is the unexpected, the seemingly irrational, which points towards God.

Thus the Logos, creator of the universe and author of scripture, used history at those many points where history actually corresponded to the hidden spiritual realities beyond history. Where such correspondence was lacking, "the scripture wove into the historical narrative what did not take place—at some points what cannot take place, and at others what can take place but did not".[2] This is to say that the ultimate author of scripture "wove into" it both myth (the impossible) and fiction (the improbable).

Presumably Origen is relying on earlier analyses of the nature of poetry, and we find in Strabo a comparable picture of the poet's work. In explaining the nature of Homer's geography, Strabo says that the poet "weaves in" some mythical elements into what is otherwise said historically and didactically.[3] The way in which the weaving takes place is more fully discussed in Aristotle's *Poetics*, where we learn that the poet is concerned with stating general truths rather than the particular facts of history.[4] "A poet's object is to tell not what actually happened but what could and would happen either probably or inevitably . . . [History] tells what happened and [poetry] what might

---

[1] A. D. Nock, *Sallustius on the Gods and the Universe* (Cambridge, 1926), xliv—xlv.
[2] *Princ.* 4. 2. 9, p. 322 Koetschau.
[3] Strabo 1. 1. 10, c. 6. [4] *Poet.* 9. 3.

happen."[1] And in convincing the audience both the marvellous and the false have their place. Indeed, "what is convincing though impossible should be preferred to what is possible and unconvincing".[2] Origen's Logos thus wrote as a good Aristotelian. The evangelists too, under the inspiration of the Logos or the Spirit, worked in the same way. They "wove into" the letter things which may seem literally false, and indeed are literally false.[3]

In the Old Testament and the New there are historical and theological impossibilities—primarily anthropomorphic descriptions of God, as in Philo—and laws which are either irrational and meaningless or impossible to obey. The exegete must therefore look for other meanings, and Origen explains the method he is to use. He should read the text carefully, looking for stumbling-blocks and seeing whether it is impossible when interpreted literally. This kind of reading was recommended by Jesus when he said, "Search the scriptures" (John 5. 39).

Next one should compare similar expressions elsewhere in scripture (presumably by using lexicons such as those the Greek grammarians compiled). In this way one can uncover allegorical meanings even in unexpected places, especially if one remembers that all scripture has a spiritual meaning. Thus the people of Israel certainly had a real history, but since Paul speaks of "Israel after the flesh" (1 Cor. 10. 18), there must be an Israel after the spirit. At this point one can consider unfulfilled prophecies about Israel and Judah. Moreover, since there is a "Jerusalem above" (Gal. 4. 26), all references to Jerusalem should be referred to the heavenly city. Indeed, this method has a universal application. If Israelites are spiritual, Egyptians and Babylonians must be spiritual too.

This analysis (in Origen's fourth book) shows that while, like other allegorizers, he can admit the historical reality of much of his text, his ultimate concern is not with history at all. Like his theology, his exegesis is fundamentally spiritual and unhistorical. He is the heir of the Greek allegorizers, of Philo, and of the gnostics. He values the Bible because it is the Church's book—that is to say, because it can be made his own book.

Origen's exegesis is based on a rigorous doctrine of verbal inspira-

---

[1] *Poet.* 9. 1, 2.   [2] Ibid., 24. 19; cf. 9. 6, 7; 24. 15, 18; 25. 27.
[3] *Ioh. comm.* 10. 5, p. 175, 10. 18–20 Preuschen.

tion. Through the Logos or the Spirit, God is the author of every detail of scripture.[1] The prophets and evangelists were instruments of the Spirit, which filled their souls. They saw and heard "in a divine fashion"; their minds were "illuminated". But while the terminology of Origen often recalls that of Philo or Josephus, he is more careful than they were to emphasize the self-consciousness and free will of the prophets.[2] For him the Spirit is not an intermittent but a permanent gift.

He clearly rejects the idea of ecstatic inspiration. Perhaps, as Zöllig suggested, he is opposing Montanist frenzy.[3] But at two points he contrasts Christian with what he calls Greek ideas. In the treatise *De principiis* he rejects the Greek doctrine that "the art of poetry cannot exist without madness", thus clearly pointing towards the doctrine of Democritus;[4] and when writing *Contra Celsum* he denounces the visceral inspiration of the Pythian priestess, arguing on Democritus' grounds that the "spirit" should have entered her through "invisible pores".[5] In this way he is claiming that biblical inspiration is more rational than that of the Greeks. Like Plato, he believes that philosophical reason is superior to the ecstasy of seers.

Origen has to hold this doctrine because of his conception of revelation as rational and of exegesis as the effort to uncover the hidden rationality. Everything in scripture is intentional. There are not some rational parts and other irrational parts. Every "jot and tittle" has a meaning which the exegete can discover if God gives him the rational power to do so.

Like Philo, Irenaeus, and Clement, Origen firmly holds that the traditional Greek translation of the Old Testament was inspired. He is unwilling to remove from it words which are not found in the Hebrew.[6] And in his late commentary on Canticles he cites two Greek versions not to correct the text but to insist that "we are certain that the Holy Spirit wanted the forms of mysteries to be hidden in the divine scripture".[7] That is to say, there are more meanings in the Septuagint text than at first appear. Moreover, since Matthew wrote

---

[1] A. Zöllig, *Die Inspirationslehre des Origenes* (Freiburg, 1903), 12-15, 58-90.
[2] Cf. *Princ.* 3. 3. 4. [3] Op. cit., 69-70.
[4] *Princ.* 3. 3. 3. p. 259, 10 Koetschau. [5] *C. Cels.* 7. 3, p. 155, 18 Koetschau.
[6] *Matt. comm.* 15. 14, p. 388 Klostermann.
[7] *Cant. comm.* I, pp. 100-1 Baehrens.

his gospel in Hebrew, its translation too was presumably inspired, even though Origen does not say so.[1]

In any event, the evangelists themselves were infallibly inspired. "None of the evangelists made an error or spoke falsely."[2] The theological reason for this infallibility is stated in the *Commentary on Matthew.* "If we believe that the gospels were accurately written with the co-operation of the Holy Spirit, those who wrote them made no errors in their remembering."[3] It might be suggested that another reason could be found in literary criticism. Without a synoptic theory, Origen had no other way to explain the passages in the synoptic gospels which are exact parallels to one another.

But the evangelists' remembering was not so much a remembrance of things past as a recognition of spiritual realities. "The apostles were eyewitnesses of the Word not because they looked at the body of the Lord and Saviour, but because they saw the Word."[4] This inner understanding, made possible by the Spirit, is far more significant than any merely historical information. Non-believers, says Origen, saw only Jesus, not Christ.[5]

Origen's doctrines of inspiration and interpretation are fused in his *Commentary on John,* his first and most important work of New Testament exegesis. Here we read that

we have now to transform the gospel known to sense-perception into one intellectual and spiritual. For what would the narrative of the gospel known to sense-perception amount to, if it were not developed into a spiritual one? It would be of little account or none. Anyone can read it and assure himself of the facts it tells—nothing more. But our whole energy is now to be directed to the effort to penetrate to the depths of the meaning of the gospel, and to search out the truth that is in it when it is divested of its prefigurations.[6]

This means that we are to treat it primarily not as a record of literal history. We are to "lift up (*anagein*) and allegorize" expressions which are seemingly meant literally.[7]

This method is partly defensive. We shall presently see that Origen

---

[1] *Matt. comm.* I, in Eusebius, *H.E.* 6. 25. 4. Papias said that there were various translations (p. 62 above), but Origen cannot accept this notion.

[2] *Ioh. comm.* 6. 34, p. 143, 25 Preuschen.   [3] *Matt. comm.* 16. 12, p. 510.

[4] *Luc. hom.* I, p. 8 Rauer.   [5] Ibid. III, pp. 22–3.

[6] *Comm.* I. 10, p. 13, 13–19 Preuschen.   [7] Ibid., I. 26, p. 33, 23.

seems to be arguing against the gospel criticisms of his predecessors, who contrasted this gospel with the synoptics. His interpretation, he claims, makes it possible to accept all four gospels rather than one, two, or three.[1] And it avoids the inadequate doctrine of inspiration implied by those who suppose that the evangelists disagree because they had poor memories.[2]

It is also in part a response to the comments on John earlier made by the Valentinian Heracleon. As de Lubac points out, Origen criticizes heretics like Heracleon for their love of allegorizing and their treatment of the healing miracles as cures of the soul alone.[3] But ordinarily Origen criticizes Heracleon's results rather than his method. Some of Origen's exegesis, as Daniélou has observed, is actually the same as that of the Valentinians.[4]

The tenth book of Origen's commentary on John provides us with two excellent examples of the boldness with which he used his exegetical method. Both are ultimately based on the disagreements among the evangelists, the first concerning the order of events at the beginning of Jesus' ministry,[5] the second concerning the times and circumstances of the cleansing of the temple.[6]

In the first instance Origen argues that the evangelists disagree when they say that God appeared to a particular person as a particular time in a particular place, that he performed a particular action and appeared in a particular form and then went away to another particular place. This statement is based on rhetorical-grammatical analyses of myth. If stories disagree on these points, it is to be presumed that they are false.[7] Origen uses this objection for a theological conclusion. The stories are not true in relation to sense-perception, for God cannot be located in space or time. They are not historical. The vision which the evangelists possessed was spiritual.

In the second instance he deals with the historical improbabilities of the story of the cleansing of the temple. "How could the son of a carpenter have dared to drive the merchant people with their doves

---

[1] Ibid., 10. 3, p. 173, 29.   [2] Ibid., 6. 34, p. 143, 29.
[3] H. de Lubac, *Histoire et Esprit* (Paris, 1950), 202.
[4] J. Daniélou, *Origène* (Paris, 1948), 190–2.
[5] *Comm.* 10. 1–5, pp. 171–5 Preuschen.   [6] Ibid., 20–34, pp. 191–208.
[7] R. M. Grant, *Miracle and Natural Law in Graeco-Roman and Early Christian Thought* (Amsterdam, 1952), 203.

and oxen from the temple? Would it not have been *hybris* for Jesus
to scatter the money of the changers and to overturn their tables? If
anyone had been struck by the scourge of cords, would he not have
fought back, especially when a whole mob of people must have
thought they had been treated unjustly? And does it not seem pre-
sumptuous and daring to assert that the Son of God took a whip and
made a scourge in order to chase people out of the temple?"[1] The
only historical fact in the narrative, says Origen, is that at festival times
merchants used to bring sacrificial animals into the outer court of the
temple. But this conclusion too is based on rhetorical-grammatical
analysis. The story is proved to be a fiction on the basis of the characters of the persons involved. In similar fashion the rhetorician Theon
shows that Medea could not have killed her children because she was
their mother, because her husband's power was greater than hers,
because she would not have committed murder publicly, and because
the motivation for the story is inadequate.[2] This method, dealing with
persons, actions, places, times, manners, and causes, can be applied to
poets' and historians' stories of gods, heroes, and mythical mixed
beings.[3] Origen is applying it to a story of one who could be classified
as either a hero or a god.

The reason for Origen's effort to prove the literal falsity of these
stories is that Gaius of Rome had endeavoured to discredit the gospel
of John by pointing out the differences between its opening chapters
and those of the synoptic gospels.[4] Origen claims that to compare
the gospel records only literally and historically is likely to lead one
to abandon the idea that the books were inspired and that their authors
were trustworthy.[5] When he has the inner meaning in view, he denies
the factual character of both John and the synoptics. There is no high
mountain such as the one to which the devil is said in the synoptics
to have taken Jesus.[6]

We must admit with de Lubac that Origen is not very consistent.
Later in the *Commentary on John* he treats the cleansing of the temple
as entirely historical, and actually refers back to his previous discussion

---

[1] Origen, *Comm.* 10. 25, summarized by S. Läuchli in *Church History* 21 (1952), 216.
[2] L. Spengel, *Rhetores graeci* II, 93-6; cf. 76-8.   [3] Ibid., 95.
[4] See Appendix III.   [5] *Comm.* 10. 3, p. 172, 21-3.
[6] *De princ.* 4. 3. 1, p. 324, 10.

without intimating that in it he had denied the historicity of the story.[1] And certainly the high mountain of Matthew and Luke could be figurative, as both Daniélou and de Lubac insist.[2]

We part company with both Daniélou and de Lubac, however, in assessing the sources and the importance of these instances in which Origen denies the historical truth of the gospel stories. Daniélou finds the principle which Origen is here applying to be Philonic and states that it is absolutely unacceptable.[3] We find it not Philonic but derived from Origen's studies of Greek grammar and rhetoric, though we agree that as a method it leaves much to be desired. De Lubac says that Origen's words should not be taken too "grossly", even though he is close to modern critics who find in the gospels a fairly "supple" kind of historicity (presumably he is referring to the words of the encyclical *Divino afflante spiritu*).[4] And he adds that "an objective study must take note" of these passages, though it would be "an injustice to emphasize them at the expense of more important and more solid characteristics of which they are only the shadow".[5] Undoubtedly these passages do not represent Origen's whole thought on this subject. They do, however, reveal the lengths to which, at least on occasion, he was willing to go in defence of the inspiration and the spiritual meaning of the gospels. In these passages Origen is revealed as the boldest allegorizer of the ancient Church.

The sources of these "bold" allegorizations do not lie in the works of Philo but, like the grammatical definitions Origen takes from the Stoic Herophilus,[6] in Greek grammar and rhetoric. His younger contemporary Porphyry pointed out this fact. According to him, Origen was always in the company of Plato, Numenius, Cronius, Apollophanes, Longinus, Moderatus, Nicomachus, and the Pythagoreans; and from the books of Chaeremon the Stoic and Cornutus he derived the metaphorical method of the Greek mysteries, applying it to the Jewish writings.[7] The evidence already cited proves that Porphyry

---

[1] H. de Lubac, *Histoire et Esprit* (Paris, 1950), 202; *Comm.* 10. 30, pp. 224-5, and 13. 56, pp. 286-7. And—and this is most important—in the *Comm. in Matt.* 16. 20 (pp. 543-4 Klostermann) he refers to his previous criticism as slavery to the letter. His mind did change.

[2] J. Daniélou, *Origène* (Paris, 1948), 181; de Lubac, op. cit., 197.

[3] Op cit., 181-2.   [4] Op. cit., 200.   [5] Ibid., 206.

[6] Cf. E. Klostermann in *ZNW* 37 (1938), 54-61.   [7] Eusebius, *H.E.* 6. 19. 8.

was not "expressing an opinion based upon a combination of unrelated things which he happened to know".[1] Jerome tells us that some of these sources were also employed in the lost *Stromateis*.[2]

Admittedly Philo was an important source of Origen's allegorization, but in rejecting the historical nature of certain passages Origen went beyond Philo. This is to say that for the negative task of detecting impossibilities or improbabilities, myths or fictions, he used Greek rhetorical analysis, even though in many instances he followed Philo in the positive work of discovering their hidden meaning.

The Greek rhetorical origin of his negative method is confirmed by a passage in the late work *Contra Celsum*, where Origen discusses Homeric exegesis "by way of introduction to the whole question of the narrative about Jesus in the gospels".[3] He states that "an attempt to substantiate (*kataskeuazein*)[4] almost any story as historical fact, even if it is true, and to produce complete certainty (*kataleptiké phantasia*) about it, is one of the most difficult tasks and in some cases is impossible". This sentence, with its allusion to the first sentence of Dio Chrysostom's oration proving the non-historical character of the *Iliad* and *Odyssey*, brings Origen to a brief discussion of mythical and fictitious elements which Homer "wove into" the true history of the Trojan war. Dio Chrysostom had actually denied that the war took place, but Origen is following the line taken by Strabo; according to him there was a real war but its history was ornamented by mythological elements.[5]

Origen concludes that "anyone who reads the stories with a fair mind and who wants to keep himself from being deceived by them, will decide what he will accept and what he will interpret allegorically (*tropologesei*), searching out the meaning of the authors who wrote such fictitious stories, and what he will disbelieve as having been written to gratify certain people". Since this is his "introduction to the question of the narrative about Jesus", it is obvious that even as

[1] H. A. Wolfson, *The Philosophy of the Church Fathers* I (Cambridge, Mass, 1956), 63.
[2] *Ep.* 70. 4, *CSEL* 54. 706.
[3] *C. Cels.* 1. 42, pp. 92–3 Koetschau (tr. Chadwick, p. 39); cf. *Miracle and Natural Law*, 199–200.
[4] A reference to the method of *kataskeué*; cf. W. Kroll in Pauly-Wissowa, *RE* Suppl. VII, 1119.
[5] Strabo 1. 2. 9, c. 20; cf. 1. 1. 10, cited above.

late as 248 he was influenced, at least sometimes, by Greek rhetorical methods.

The significance of Origen's work as an allegorizer is to be found precisely at this point. Where Clement was content to follow Philo and the Stoics in allegorizing ancient texts which made theological statements "unworthy of God", Origen went on to examine the truth or falsity of fairly recent historical narratives, and to argue, when he had shown that some of them were false, that they contained a higher, spiritual truth. This argument was made necessary by his fundamental assumptions of the inerrancy of the evangelists and of the primacy of the spiritual in relation to the merely historical.

No allegorizer before him had gone so far. What he had done was to treat the gospels in the way in which he had treated (following Philo and the Valentinians) the creation story in Genesis. Genesis contains stories of the impossible (i.e., myths) such as the mention of "days" before the creation of sun and moon. The gospels contain stories of the same kind. And in dealing with the disagreements among the gospels, Origen proceeded to explain, on the basis of Greek rhetorical methods, exactly why the stories were to be regarded as impossible.

This is only one aspect of his allegorical method. It is not an aspect which he himself may have regarded as supremely important, and he did not consistently apply the principles involved. But without this use of negative historical criticism it is hard to see what rational justification Origen could have provided for allegorizing the historical narratives of the New Testament.

If we now ask what the basic presuppositions of the allegorical school were, we shall find them closely correlated, as we should expect, with their general world-view. For all the allegorizers the world is essentially comprehensible by philosophical reason. The ancient writers were rational and really wrote philosophy. However, they used allegory in order to conceal their meaning for didactic or political purposes; alternatively, poets added allegory simply in order to provide pleasure. By means of what may be called de-allegorizing it is possible to get back to their true and original meaning. For Philo the situation is more complicated, since he is not only a philosopher but also a Jew. He believes in God's creative acts, in miracles, and in ecstatic inspiration. God reveals himself not only in the ordinary course of nature, as in philosophical thought, but also in some miraculous alterations of nature and in irrational revelations. However, as a philosopher Philo believes that the totality of being is ultimately rational and he therefore interprets seeming irrationalities in the light of reason. The most general is the most true. For this reason the specific histories of the patriarchs are explained away so that they become the inner history of every man.

The Christian Platonists of Alexandria make use of Philonic ideas but take history more seriously. Clement, on the one hand, comes closer to ordinary allegorizers and philosophers with his insistence on the didactic importance of allegorical expressions and the necessity for keeping secrets from the profane. Origen, on the other, combines Philonic emphasis on revelation in nature and in scripture with a stress on the cleavage between historical events and written gospels. By severely limiting the possible or the actual, he leaves even more room for the rôle of the creative but rational imagination, due to the Holy Spirit, in the writing of scripture. Nothing was written without purpose. Thus on the one hand the evangelists could remember everything and recorded everything correctly; on the other, they often presented as perceptible to the senses events which were known by the mind alone. It seems likely that as he grew older Origen adhered less closely to his basic theory as set forth in the *De principiis* and reflected in the *Commentary on John*. These two works, however, are the high-water mark of allegorization in the ancient Church.

The method itself obviously leaves something to be desired. In arguing against opponents whom they regarded as crude literalists, the allegorizers showed that many biblical passages are metaphorical. They were unwilling, however, to say that the metaphorical meaning was in fact the literal meaning of these passages. In a metaphorical expression they found two meanings, the literal and the spiritual, and they went on to find both meanings in non-metaphorical statements. Yet by this means, imperfect as it was, they were able to translate the gospels, at least in part, into terms meaningful in their own environment. They were able to pass from the letter of the Bible to the spirit by which it was inspired.

6

THE LETTER AND THE SPIRIT

W E need not trace the refinements of allegorization to be found among later Christian exegetes, or even discuss the more sober and literal exegesis of scripture developed by the exegetical school of Antioch. At Antioch there was a much stronger feeling for the human element in the biblical writers and a better understanding of the historical reality of the biblical revelation. This emphasis was brought about by several important factors—a closer relationship to Jewish exegesis, the influence of Aristotelian rather than Platonic philosophy, and (in the light of both these points) the development of a theology concerned as much with the humanity as with the divinity of Christ.

At the same time, the difference between Alexandria and Antioch can be exaggerated, and at Antioch too there is a high doctrine of inspiration. Allegorization is not entirely absent. In practice, as contrasted with theory, the two kinds of exegesis come together.

Our concern, however, is with the theory which lies behind the development of allegorization in the early Church. And we cannot be content simply to describe this development without analysing the theory and indicating its strengths and weaknesses.

The greatest strength of the allegorizers' theory lies in its insistence that God speaks through the writings of prophets and apostles. At times the allegorizers stress the divine origin of inspiration to such an extent that they obliterate the human element in the writing of scripture. But if they were to maintain that God (or the gods) spoke to men through the writings, they had to hold that revelation was not given simply in events; the poets and prophets who wrote were themselves instruments of revelation.

Moreover, the allegorizers were convinced that the revelation had meaning not only in the past but in the present. If God (or the gods) gave revelation to great men of the past, this revelation possessed hidden meanings which could be understood directly by men of later times. There might be a progressive development of men's understanding of the revelation, but this understanding was not likely to surpass that which great poets and prophets had been given. In this regard, at least, the allegorizers had a healthy sense of humility.

They were also aware that poets and prophets had been given a source of inspiration which seemed to be more than human. The poet's treatment of his theme was not simply a result of skill or art. His inspiration came from something or someone outside himself. And he was able to reach levels of understanding beyond those accessible to ordinary persons. The extension of inspiration to the evangelists meant that the evangelists were regarded not as simple compilers of tradition but as creative writers whose memories were moved by a power beyond them. In other words, the evangelists at the very least selected their materials and gave them the form or shape which is found in the gospels. In this respect Origen marks an advance over Papias. Papias had said that Mark wrote down everything he heard. Origen more adequately recognizes that Mark, like the other evangelists, was to some extent a creator. He ascribes Mark's creative power to the Holy Spirit.

Because of this creative power, which could not be analysed in purely literary or historical terms, poets, prophets, and evangelists wrote works which continued to have meaning long after they were written. These works were at least classics; at most they were scripture. There is a considerable degree of truth in the adage, "They were inspiring and therefore inspired".

Moreover, because of poetic and prophetic use of symbolic language, there was a vagueness (partly deliberate) about their meaning, and its interpretation also required a kind of "divination". Religious writers, trying to express realities ultimately supra-rational, did not express their intuitions in terms of definitions or arguments. They proclaimed revelation in obscure metaphorical language, which could be understood only by others whose thought moved along similar lines. To take a metaphor "literally" or verbally was to destroy the power it possessed for giving insight into the mysteries of God. To take it "spiritually" was to use it as a guide to transcendent levels of meaning.

This much can be said in defence of the allegorizers. We should recognize that they were not dishonestly trying to use the poets and the prophets as cloaks for their own philosophical speculations. They believed that they had come to know the truth, the ultimate truth which lay behind the poets, the prophets, and the philosophers. They therefore insisted on the oneness of truth and found, to their own satisfaction, that it was expressed in one way in poetry or scripture and in another way in philosophy. Behind both forms of expression lay revelation.

On the other hand, because of their reverence for philosophy, they tended to empty history of meaning. History was at best an imperfect representation of eternal truth. Since they concentrated their attention on the timeless reality of God, temporal events could only be shadows of heavenly images. When they emphasized the myths of the aeons, or even spoke of the reality of the Incarnation, they could not see God's working in specific historical events. Events were merely symbols of eternal truth.

At this point the allegorizers betrayed the intentions of the authors with whom they were dealing. Neither Homer nor Hesiod viewed his own writings as timeless in this way, and the biblical writers speak of a God who actively creates the universe and governs history, revealing himself not only through the oracles of his prophets but also in events. Thus it is the Incarnation, not a philosophical conception of God, which is the foundation of Christian theology, even though a philosophical conception of God is also involved.

When allegorizers came to explain how it was that they possessed the true key to the meaning of ancient writings, they took two different lines of approach. There were those who held that there was a true ancient theology which had been corrupted and interpolated by poets and priests; they themselves, by removing these additional elements, were able to recover it. Again, there were those who regarded the whole tradition as expressed in symbolic language, and by interpreting it allegorically were able to penetrate to its inner meaning. Some of these interpreters used the method of etymologizing; others relied on a secret tradition of exegesis; still others insisted on the guidance of the Spirit in their work. In the interpretations of all of them there was a considerable element of subjectivity. The recovery of the ancient theology was largely a matter of conjecture, and the assigning of precise rational meanings to the old symbols necessarily required the treatment of them as less fluid than they were.

But the basic difficulty with the allegorizers' work lay in their presupposition of the absolute infallibility and authority of ancient documents. This presupposition, expressed by many of them, is set forth by Augustine.[1]

> If we are perplexed by an apparent contradiction in scripture, it is not permissible to say, The author of this book is mistaken; instead, the manuscript is faulty, or the translation is wrong, or you have not understood. . . . Scripture has a sacredness peculiar to itself. In other books the reader may form his own opinion and perhaps, from not understanding the writer, may differ from him. . . . We are bound to receive as true whatever the canon shows to have been said by even one prophet or apostle or evangelist.

Under these conditions the allegorical method becomes an escape mechanism. The exegete, unwilling to admit that contradictions exist, flees to the refuge provided by a higher spiritual truth.

Has a more satisfactory solution of these difficulties been provided in modern times? Certainly both ancient approaches to the problem have been followed. In the first place, modern New Testament scholars, using the method of Cornutus, Philo of Byblos, and Marcion, have believed that they could disentangle an authentic primitive teaching from later distortions. Thus Harnack, in *Das Wesen des Christentums* (1900), found a core of teaching which was not only authentic but also immediately meaningful to liberal theologians at the turn of the century. Jesus proclaimed the Fatherhood of God, the brotherhood of man, and the value of the individual soul. Harnack's contemporary, P. W. Schmiedel, discovered what he called "pillar passages" in the teaching of Jesus, that is to say passages which contradicted later ecclesiastical teaching and therefore could not have been invented by the evangelists. W. Wrede argued that the injunctions to secrecy about the Messiahship of Jesus reflected a dogmatic theory of the evangelist Mark, and he went on to claim that Jesus actually did not regard himself as the Messiah.[2] These notions, characteristic of the liberal school at its peak, are close to the grammatical theories of the ancients.

Others have taken Pauline doctrine to be the true New Testament

---

[1] *Contra Faustum Manichaeum* 11. 5; other examples in W. Sanday, *Inspiration* (London, 1893), 36–8.

[2] Later critics asked whether the term Messiah had any fixed meaning.

teaching, and have criticized other parts of the New Testament in relation to it.[1] This kind of treatment is provided in Dibelius' discussion of the speech on the Areopagus ascribed to Paul (Acts 17. 22–31):

> The speech is alien to the New Testament (apart from Acts 14. 15–17), as it is familiar to Hellenistic, particularly Stoic, philosophy. . . . The speaker on the Areopagus is the precursor of the Apologists. But the Church followed them and not Paul. . . . The magnitude of this change cannot easily be overestimated, for the whole of ecclesiastical theology was affected by it.[2]

Here the, or an, interpolator is clearly identified as the author of Acts, who invented the speech on the Areopagus and thus distorted primitive doctrine:

> Luke strayed too far from the Paul who was the theologian of the paradoxes of grace and faith; nevertheless, he gave for the future the signal for the Christian message to be spread abroad by means of Hellenistic culture.[3]

The concession provided by the second half of Dibelius' sentence does not go far enough, for it must be remembered that the New Testament does not consist solely of Paul; it includes the Areopagus speech as well.

In any event, the method of *Formgeschichte*, in which Dibelius himself was a pioneer, undermined the liberal theory of interpolations in the gospels. This method, which came to the fore at the end of the First World War, consisted of studying the items of oral tradition which circulated before the gospels were written. Its users treated the framework of the gospels as a late invention, intended merely to hold the fragments of tradition together. But as their studies proceeded, they came to recognize that the whole tradition, to a greater or lesser degree, was the product of the early Church and was modified and shaped by the Church in various situations. Bultmann tried to distinguish authentic Jewish elements from fictitious Hellenistic

---

[1] This notion goes back beyond Luther to Marcion, as Harnack observed.
[2] M. Dibelius, *Studies in the Acts of the Apostles* (New York, 1956), 63.
[3] Ibid., 77. Dibelius also distinguishes "the real core of the Pauline message" from "the hortatory passages of the Pauline epistles", which were "not composed by Paul" but simply adapted by him, largely from "Hellenistic thought" (p. 59).

elements, but later studies of first-century Judaism have shown that these elements cannot be clearly differentiated.

This development means that the search for an uninterpolated tradition has led to recognition that the interpolations cannot so easily be separated from the tradition as a whole. The study of the gospels therefore passed once more from the hands of grammarians to those of theologians. A product of the transition is the commentary of the Fourth Gospel by Bultmann, both grammarian and theologian. In it he believes he can find a primitive source-document employed by the evangelist and finally interpolated by an ecclesiastical redactor. The source-document can be interpreted in modern existential theological terms. Yet for many theologians this method is unsatisfactory. Their reaction is expressed by E. C. Blackman:[1]

> There is something worth pondering in the remark of Ehrenburg (quoted by Jenkins . . .) that if you wish to find the Holy Spirit in the Bible you look first in passages marked R (Redactor) by the critics.

This remark corresponds to certain elements in the history of Christian theology, which in a way is a history of interpolation or at least of reinterpretation. From the ancient period we need only cite the mass of literature ascribed to Clement, Ignatius, and Dionysius the Areopagite, not to mention the Pastoral Epistles, or, to go farther back, to the composition of the Pentateuch or the writings of the prophets.

The conflict between those who have looked for non-interpolated tradition and those who have reinterpreted the tradition as a whole is analogous to the difference between the left-wing and liberal Protestant demand for the restoration of primitive doctrine and the Catholic feeling for continuity and the authority of the Church, shared to a considerable extent by right-wing Protestants.

The appeal of writers like Irenaeus to the apostolic tradition as handed down and interpreted in the apostolic succession is meaningful within the context of Catholic Churches which stress the continuity of Christian experience and do not regard Church history as the story of distortion and interpolation. Within such Churches there is an emphasis on the unity of truth and a search for various senses which

[1] W. D. Davies and D. Daube, *The Background of the New Testament and its Eschatology* (Cambridge, 1956), 9 n. 2.

a scriptural passage can have. There is what might be called a con-
servative recognition of the ambiguity of language. In modern Roman
Catholicism this recognition is reflected in the discussion of the *sensus
plenior*.[1]

Protestants too appeal to the apostolic tradition, but they have
tended to limit its meaning to the literal sense of scripture, and among
liberal Protestants there has been widespread use of theories of interpolation. It has been believed that biblical critics, using purely
objective methods, could lay bare the history of interpolation. But
the rise of the form-critical method suggested that previous investiga-
tions were not as objective as they seemed. In a sense, everything in
the gospels is an interpolation, for the whole tradition about Jesus
was transmitted and modified by the Church. More recently there
has been greater emphasis on the creative originality of the evangelists
themselves. They were not merely transmitters of tradition but
editors to whom the Church owed its portraits of Jesus.

Here, as Brown has pointed out, there is a correlation between
Catholic and Protestant theory. He cites the words of Coppens:[2]

> The words of Jesus . . . have since the beginning been so rich in meaning
> and possibilities that each one of the four Gospels could refract particular
> aspects of them. The traditions behind the four Gospels reflect four
> successive stages of New Testament theological thought, giving an exact
> rendition of the authentic nuances in the Master's thought. The Evangel-
> ists have developed the *sensus plenior* of these words of Christ; and the
> charism of inspiration guarantees the fidelity of this development of the
> original.

The *sensus plenior* which Brown defines and advocates is not very
different from the allegorical meaning found by Origen. Brown provides this definition:[3]

> The *sensus plenior* is that additional, deeper meaning, intended by God
> but not clearly intended by the human author, which is seen to exist in
> the words of a biblical text (or group of texts, or even a whole book)
> when they are studied in the light of further revelation or development
> in the understanding of revelation.

Origen, however, did not regard the allegorical or spiritual meaning
as something "additional", and at least in the case of the evangelists

---

[1] R. E. Brown, *The Sensus Plenior of Sacred Scripture* (Baltimore, 1955).
[2] Ibid., 144–5.   [3] Ibid., 92.

he believed that it was clearly intended by the inspired author, in full possession of his rational faculties. On the other hand, he would have agreed with Brown that "the full meaning of the New Testament was [not] immediately evident to the early Christians".[1] And he would have recognized, at least in theory, the force of the appeal to the guidance of the Church and the Fathers.[2]

The basic difference between advocates of a *sensus plenior* and historical critics is perhaps not so much theological as philosophical. It can be compared to the difference in modern Protestant theology between Tillich, with his concern for ontology, and Niebuhr, with his emphasis on history. As Will Herberg points out, "Where Tillich asserts that 'all problems drive us to an ontological analysis', Niebuhr insists that 'the human person and man's society are by nature historical, and the ultimate truth about life must be mediated historically'."[3] At this point the "presuppositionless" grammarian and historical critic sides with Niebuhr, and the allegorizing advocate of the *sensus plenior* is likely to side with Tillich. The historical critic endeavours to find out what the ancient author meant and to fit his intention into the context of the historical process, while the allegorizer tries to discover the permanent ontological meaning latent in the text.

Unfortunately the historian often seems to believe that simply to search for facts is to perform a theological task, while the theologian tries to by-pass or short-circuit historical data. And in the course of the debate between them each tends to parody the position of the other while claiming a monopoly of insight for himself. At this point there is needed a doctrine of the Church in which various members have various functions and there is a continuing conversation about the relation of history to faith. For this conversation no specific rules of order can be laid down.

Yet the memory of Origen can provide insights which may illuminate the path such a conversation should follow. He believed in the complete and rational inspiration of the evangelists. This is to say, as many modern critics believe, that they were creative writers, who controlled and shaped the materials with which they dealt. He was

[1] Op. cit., 93.   [2] Ibid., 145–6.
[3] *Union Seminary Quarterly Review* 11, 4 (May 1956), 14.

critically aware of the differences between them, and believed that these differences could be accounted for not on the basis of source criticism or a search for interpolations but in relation to their ultimate purpose as evangelists. He claimed that they were concerned not so much with literal historical fact as with the revelation in history of ontological truth. Here he would agree with Dibelius' statement about Luke: "The 'historical' dilemma no longer exists if we do not regard Luke's compilation as history, at least not as history which took place in accordance with this sequence of events. Here, as elsewhere, Luke has abandoned an exact reproduction of history for the sake of a higher historical truth."[1] Such a statement narrows the gap between historians and theologians and turns both towards the search for that "higher historical truth" for which ancient allegorizers, with all their limitations, were seeking.

But what is "a higher historical truth"? Dibelius tells us that in Acts it "consists of the idea that the incorporating of the Gentiles into the Church without subjecting them to the law originated neither with Paul, nor with Peter, but with God". Admittedly it is difficult to separate fact from interpretation, in the New Testament as elsewhere, but it seems difficult to regard the divine origin of gentile freedom from Jewish law as historical rather than theological truth. Dibelius implicitly admits this difficulty when he advocates the consideration of "Luke's compilation" not as history but as something else. Theologically, it is true to say that Luke's conception originated with God. Historically, however, it originated with Paul or with Peter or with some other human being. And at this point the languages of theology and of history diverge. The theologian and the historical critic must recognize the autonomy, at least relative, of their disciplines; they can seek for areas of agreement while admitting that their functions are different. A thoroughly theological history is no history at all, while a merely historical theology is not theology.

It was the error of the ancient allegorizers to try to combine history with theology in such a way that history was ultimately emptied of meaning. Interpolation theories, on the other hand, were attempts to make historical sense of historical documents, but they failed because of their arbitrary character. It remains to be seen whether modern

[1] Op. cit., 122.

theologians and historical critics can avoid the errors of their fore-runners.

Perhaps the solution will be found in wider employment of the term "myth", though this term is dangerous because of the suspicion of falsity attached to it both in ancient and in modern times. Origen, as we have seen, does not use the term though he certainly finds myth, or rather myths, in the gospels. But the language of a historical religion, that is to say, a religion which speaks of God's working in history, must of necessity combine history with theology. In this language we should expect to find expressions such as "God said" and "God did", expressions whose truth cannot be verified empirically. It is a language of pictures and symbols, not of pictures and symbols alone, but of concrete historical facts such as "in the year that king Uzziah died" (Isa. 6. 1) or "in the fifteenth year of Tiberius Caesar" (Luke 3. 1). What happened in these years? In the year Uzziah died "I saw the Lord", and in the fifteenth year of Tiberius "the word of God came to John". There is an indissoluble mixture of theology and history, a mixture which can be called "myth" until some better term is found. Each in his own way, the theologian and the historian can try to do justice to this mixture, even though the emphases of each will provide results unlike, or at least not identical with, those of the other. Within the context of the Christian community, each will be trying to make intelligible the gospel which the Church proclaims.

APPENDIX I

MARCION'S GOSPEL

The purpose of this appendix is to show that Marcion presumably corrected the Gospel of Luke in the light of his own peculiar doctrines. He did not possess an "original gospel" and his philology is only a weapon for his theology.

We do not possess a great deal of reliable information about his gospel. The most important sources are Tertullian and Epiphanius. In the fourth book of his treatise *Against Marcion*, written between 207 and 212, Tertullian goes through Marcion's Luke to show that it confirms orthodox doctrine. The passages to which he does not refer were probably, though not certainly, omitted by Marcion. Epiphanius, writing about 374, had earlier made excerpts from Marcion's gospel to show that in it could be found (*a*) the agreement of the two testaments, (*b*) the reality of the Incarnation, (*c*) the resurrection of the dead, and (*d*) the oneness of God. He also included passages which Marcion regarded as interpolations; and therefore we cannot use Epiphanius' testimony except when he says that Marcion "deleted" a passage. Only about half of the seventy-seven Epiphanius gives are really relevant.

The best way to recover Marcion's gospel is to deal first with those passages which Tertullian and Epiphanius explicitly say he deleted, and to classify them in relation to what we know of Marcion's theology. Thus there are twenty-three such passages, to be classified as follows:

1. References to the Father as Creator (12. 6, 7) or as the God of Abraham, Isaac, and Jacob (20. 37, 38);
2. References to prophecy or to the Old Testament generally (3. 1b—4. 30; 11. 29b-32; 11. 49-51; 17. 10b; 18. 31-3; 24. 27; 24. 44-6);
3. References implying concern for the Jews (13. 1-9; 15. 11-32; 19. 9b; 19. 29-46; 20. 9-18; 21. 21-4; 22. 16) or implying that Jesus was the warrior messiah of the Jews (22. 35-8; 22. 50);
4. References implying resurrection of the body (12. 28; 21. 18) or immediate entrance to Paradise (23. 43); and
5. The story of the human birth and growth of Jesus (1. 1-2. 52,

including his visit to his Father's house at Jerusalem) and mention of his mother and brothers (8. 19).

We assume that 24. 27 and 24. 44–6 were deleted since Marcion certainly removed 18. 31–3.

John Knox (*Marcion and the New Testament*, Chicago, 1942, 85, 86), who holds that Marcion knew a primitive form of Luke, asks: "Why should Marcion have omitted the parable of the Prodigal Son, or the story of the massacre of the Galileans, or the conversation in which the Pharisees tell Jesus that Herod wishes to kill him?"

The answer to the first question may be that the parable of the Prodigal Son (Luke 15. 11–32) teaches, as Irenaeus (*Adv. haer.* 4. 36. 7) says, that the two sons have one and the same Father. Tertullian (*De cast.* 8) states that "some find in the two sons the two peoples, the elder being the Jewish and the younger the Christian". Marcion could not have accepted such exegesis.

The answer to the second question may be that the massacre of the Galileans seems to imply that God is neither just nor loving, and Marcion could not have agreed. Moreover he deleted the parable of the fig tree, immediately following (Luke 13. 6–9), which leaves room for hope for the Jews (cf. Tertullian, *Res. carn.* 33). He could well have omitted a doubtful passage with one definitely unsatisfactory.

The answer to the third question is that Luke 13. 31 is part of a larger context partly omitted, partly emended. Marcion removed a reference to patriarchs and prophets as in the kingdom of God as well as a lament over Jerusalem. There was no reason to retain a reference to friendly Pharisees, who after all were Jews.

Knox argues that Marcion's omissions come primarily from Luke's special materials, and that therefore these materials may have been added after Marcion's time. By counting verses (op. cit., 107) he reaches a figure of nearly eighty per cent from "special Luke". It may be replied that (*a*) his theological motives account for the omissions, and (*b*) if we count sections rather than verses the figure is reduced to fifty per cent. Was Marcion concerned with words and phrases or with ideas?

If we next turn to Marcion's minor alterations and omissions, we find three changes which apparently have no theological significance.

In Luke 9. 41 he read *pros autous* instead of *autois*, a grammatical change without significance. And in Luke 10. 22 and 12. 38 his text agreed with the ordinary "Western" text of the second century as represented by Codex Bezae. On the other hand, there are fifteen alterations where theological motivation seems evident.

    1. Passages referring to the Highest God as compared with the Creator and his angels (10. 21; 12. 8; 12. 32; 18. 19);

    2. Passages relating the Old Testament to the gospel (22. 20; 23. 2; 24. 25) or favouring the law (16. 17);

    3. Passages apparently favouring the Jews (5. 14; 13. 28–35);

    4. Passages implying that the Jewish idea of resurrection is Christian (10. 25); or mentioning the judgement (11. 42: *klesin* for *krisin*);

    5. Passages implying that Jesus was human (6. 17); and

    6. Passages involving asceticism, which Marcion favoured (11. 2: an addition to the Lord's prayer; 23. 2: an addition to the charges against Jesus, based on 14. 26).

It is difficult to believe that all these changes were not motivated solely by theological factors.

Furthermore, we must consider Marcion's exegesis of his gospel in order to see whether or not the same ideas are operative. Here too the same points are found.

    1. The Father of Jesus is not the Creator-god of the Jews, served by John the Baptist (4. 35; 5. 33–5; 8. 24; 10. 22; 11. 1; 11. 5–8; 12. 1; 12. 39; 16. 19–31; 20. 35; 21. 17);

    2. Jesus rejected the law and the prophets (4. 32; 5. 27; 6. 9; 8. 47–8; 16. 16–18);

    3. Jesus rejected the Jews (7. 9; 11. 19), and predicted that they would persecute his apostles (21. 17); he was not the warrior messiah (9. 21; 18. 38; 21. 9–11; 22. 67–70);

    4. Jesus predicted a spiritual resurrection (14. 16); and

    5. Jesus was not human (4. 31; 8. 20; 22. 19; 24. 39).

Other points which Marcion emphasized were the novelty of the gospel (5. 36–8; 6. 20–49; 10. 9; 10. 21) and the primacy of faith (7. 50; 8. 48).

At two points he did not delete enough. Luke 20. 35 refers to "those who are accounted worthy to attain to that age and the resurrection from the dead". Marcion took this verse to mean "those who are accounted worthy by the god of that age to attain to the resurrection of the dead". Presumably he had in mind 2 Cor. 4. 4, a verse of which he made much (cf. Irenaeus 3. 7. 1, 2). Again, Luke 24. 39 represents Jesus as saying: "A spirit does not have flesh and bones such as you see me having." Marcion dropped "flesh and", and reversed the word order: "A spirit, such as you see me having, does not have bones." In each case he could argue that the Greek text contains at least an element of ambiguity. From such a small seed came the tree of his exegesis.

Now if we finally turn to passages not discussed by Tertullian and therefore probably omitted by Marcion, we find essentially the same situation.

1. No passages concerning the Father and the Creator are in this group, though there is one which praises John the Baptist (7. 29–35).

2. There are passages which relate the Old Testament to the gospel so explicitly that we have already included them as certain omissions (24. 27; 24. 44–6).

3. Passages apparently favouring the Jews (8. 41, 42; 8. 49–56 [daughter of the synagogue-chief]; 10. 12–15 [woes on gentile cities]; 10. 26, 28 [commending the law]; 19. 47, 48 [teaching in the temple]; 21. 1–4 [approval of the widow's temple-offering]; 23. 27–31 [lament of the people of Jerusalem]; 23. 34b–38 [Jesus as king of the Jews]). Jesus was not the warrior messiah or king (14. 31, 32; 19. 27, 28).

4. There can hardly be drinking from a cup in the kingdom of God (22. 17, 18).

5. Voluntary poverty (12. 33, 34; 18. 24–30) is not the gospel ideal. Perhaps Marcion, a wealthy man, was opposed to voluntary poverty; or perhaps he regarded it as irrelevant compared with asceticism.

Two other passages are hard to classify. Marcion apparently left out the parable of the Good Samaritan (10. 30–7) and the Lord's preference for Mary rather than Martha (10. 38–42). We may suggest that perhaps Tertullian did not mention them because he could not prove anything from them, and that Marcion did include them in his gospel. Alternatively, Marcion may not have liked the Samaritan's helping someone who went from Jerusalem to Jericho (10. 30). The story is too simple and earthly. Origen later said that the journey was that of Adam from Paradise to the world (*Luc. hom.* 34). And if Martha represented the Synagogue and Mary the Church (Origen, cf. H. Smith, *Ante-Nicene Exegesis of the Gospels*, IV, London, 1928, 54, 55), Marcion may have thought the Synagogue was treated too well.

In spite of some points hard to explain, it seems clear that Marcion was no textual, literary, or historical critic except in so far as he used criticism to bolster up his theological conclusions. He took the Gospel of Luke and ruthlessly edited it to suit his own doctrines.

APPENDIX II
GREEK EXEGETICAL TERMINOLOGY

In order to round out our treatment of allegorization, we include the following discussion of the principal terms used by non-Christians and Christians alike. Its primary purpose is to support our claim that there is a direct line of continuity between Greek and Christian exegesis.

1. ainigma

Ancient writers express their thought "enigmatically" (in the form of an *ainigma*); they "hint at" (*ainissesthai*) what they mean—or so allegorizers say. The noun, often used by Greek authors to refer to the utterances of oracles (Kittel in *TW* I 177), is found with *parabolé* in Deut. 28. 37; Sirach 39. 3; 47. 15. It is relatively rare in Philo, who speaks of scripture as full of unclarity and "enigmas" (*Leg. all.* 3. 226), and argues that therefore one must use the allegorical method (ibid. 231). Dreams too contain enigmas (*Somn.* 2. 3, 4) and must be interpreted the same way. An "enigmatic" word contains symbols (*Spec.* 1. 200).

This is the usage we find in the Greek allegorizers. Strabo (Poṣidonius?) 474 says that "accurate solution of all enigmas is not easy". Heraclitus (the allegorizer) says that Heraclitus (the philosopher) "speaks allegorically in his whole enigmatic treatment of nature" (37. 13, Teubner ed.); this treatment involves the use of symbols (37. 6, 7). Cornutus speaks of the ancients as "philosophizing through symbols and enigmas" (76. 4, 5, Lang). This was also the practice of the poets. Those who transmitted myths spoke enigmatically (28. 1; 32. 14; 62. 11). This was a common view: Plutarch (*Pyth.* 407 b), Celsus (Origen, *C. Cels.* 6. 42), Maximus of Tyre (*Diss.* 4. 5a, Hobein), and Porphyry (*De Styge* ap. Stob. *Ecl.* 2. 1. 19) state that enigmas are characteristic of ancient poets and oracles.

Some grammarians were not enthusiastic about enigmas. Trypho (*Rhet. graeci* III 193. 14, Spengel) says that "it is a form of expression arranged with the wrongful purpose of concealing the meaning in unclarity, or setting forth something impossible or impracticable".

He explains that while allegory is obscure in either expression or thought, enigma is obscure in both. Similarly, Quintilian (*Inst.* 8. 6. 52) calls it "a more obscure allegory". The terms were not always kept distinct, however; in reworking a common source Pseudo-Plutarch uses one, Heraclitus the other (K. Reinhardt, *De graecorum theologia quaestiones duae*, Berlin, 1910, 20).

Among Christian writers it is first used in an exegetical sense by Justin, who employs the verb in relation to Plato's mysterious speech (allegory) about the universe (*Dial.* 5. 4) and Daniel's about the Son of Man (76. 1). Probably influenced by the Greek Bible, the *Preaching of Peter* (Clement, *Str.* 6. 128. 1) says that the prophets spoke in parables and enigmas. Among the Valentinians, too, it is correlated with "parable" (Clement, *Exc. Theod.* 66), and the verb is used to describe the language of Genesis (*Exc.* 57. 4; 51. 2), Matthew (61. 5), and the Gospel of the Egyptians (67. 4). Origen also associates it with parable (*Luc. hom.* 268 LXX 3, Rauer).

Clement uses it of hieroglyphics (*Str.* 5. 41. 2) and of the writings of the prophets (*Protr.* 10. 1; *Str.* 5. 55. 3). The truth, he says, has been delivered in enigmas and symbols (*Str.* 5. 21. 4). Origen uses it in his *Commentary on John* as the equivalent of symbol (59. 24, Preuschen) or allegory (106. 19; 140. 27; 145. 35; 151. 16; 201. 17; 206. 13; 235. 4). Once it is a hint or veiled allusion (347. 5). In *Contra Celsum* (i. 101. 23), however, he distinguishes it from allegory. This distinction is also found in the grammarians we have mentioned, and in Josephus (*Ant.* 1. 24), who says that Moses used enigma, allegory, and plain language.

2. *allegoria*

This word is a product of the rhetorical schools of the first century B.C. Though it is sometimes attributed to Cleanthes, it occurs only in a late indirect testimony to his teaching (*SVF* I. 526). The earliest examples occur in Philodemus (*Rhet.* i. 164. 22; 174. 24), where the "tropes" metaphor and allegory are differentiated. The adjective and adverb appear in Demetrius (*Eloc.* 282, 243), and the noun is used by Dionysius of Halicarnassus in a treatise against Demetrius (cited in *Ep. ad Pomp.* 2, p. 98, Roberts).

Allegory is a continuous metaphor, as Cicero says (*Orator* 94; *De*

THE LETTER AND THE SPIRIT

orat. 3. 166). Like enigma, it can be used to mislead (cf. Cicero, *Ad Att.* 2. 20. 3); the plural can mean *"paroles sans suite"* (A. D. Nock and A. J. Festugière, *Hermès Trismégiste* IV, Paris, 1954, 95 n. 65). Writings had of course been allegorized long before Philo, but he is the first to make frequent use of the word *allegoria*, e.g., in *Abr.* 131, *Jos.* 28, *Dec.* 1, *Spec.* 2. 29, 147, *Praem.* 125. He associates it with symbols, tropes, and enigma, and says that "most of the (Mosaic) legislation is expressed allegorically" (*Jos.* 28). He frequently uses the word with *physikōs*, which in this context can be translated as "really". The allegorizer Heraclitus uses the verb twenty-five times, the noun nineteen times, and the adjective fifteen times. Quintilian defines it as a continuous metaphor tending towards enigma (*Inst.* 8. 6. 14; 9. 2. 46) or an "inversion meaning one thing in language, another in sense" (8. 6. 44). The latter definition is also found in Heraclitus.

The word was therefore common in the first century, and H. de Lubac (*Histoire et Esprit*, Paris, 1950, 22 n. 1) seems to be mistaken in saying that when Paul used it, it was still a neologism. He cites Plutarch, *Aud. poet.* 4, who refers to *"hyponoiai,* now called *allegoriai"*. What Plutarch probably means is that the earlier term is Platonic (cf. *Def. orac.* 414f.). And Plutarch is not discussing Heraclitus, whose exegesis was different from that which he describes. The grammarian Cornutus does not use the word, perhaps because it was a term of abuse as in Philo of Byblos.

Among Christian writers the first to use the word is the apostle Paul, who speaks (Gal. 4. 24) of Sarah and Hagar, or the stories about them, as "meant allegorically". He could have said that the stories were allegories, for the term itself does not suggest that the stories are fictitious; it simply means that the obvious meaning is not the basic one.

In the apostolic fathers, as in the rest of the New Testament, the word is absent. The adjective occurs in Aristides, *Apol.* 13. 7, in reference to Greek treatment of myths. The noun is found in a fragment of Justin preserved in Irenaeus (*Adv. haer.* 5. 26. 2) but omitted by Eusebius (*H.E.* 4. 18) when he quotes Justin from Irenaeus (the words in italics are omitted by Eusebius): "Before the Lord's coming, Satan never ventured to blaspheme God; since he did not yet know of his own condemnation, *for it was latent in parables and allegories.*"

Since Justin elsewhere avoids the word, we may perhaps suppose that he was impressed by Marcion's refusal to "allegorize" the Old Testament (Origen, *Matt. comm.* 356. 27, Klostermann; A. v. Harnack, *Marcion: das Evangelium vom fremden Gott*, ed. 2, Leipzig, 1924, 260*). Another example from the apologists occurs in Tatian, who urges the Greeks not to allegorize their myths and gods, and speaks of the foolishness of Metrodorus, who "transferred everything to allegory" (*Or.* 21; cf. W. Nestle in *Philologus* 66 (1907), 503–8, and W. den Boer in *Vigiliae christianae* 1 (1947), 156–8). Like Marcion, Celsus criticizes some Christians for allegorizing and says that their allegories are more preposterous and shameful than the Greek myths (Origen, *C. Cels.* 1. 27; 4. 51).

Valentinians did not hesitate to use the word: Theodotus (*Exc.* 56. 5) follows Philo (*Abr.* 57, etc.) in treating "Israel" as an allegory of the one who sees God, and said that "the prophecy [of Moses] spoke allegorically, in the case of Adam, of the soul as 'bone'" (*Exc.* 62. 2, Gen. 2. 23).

Clement frequently employs both noun and verb, relating allegory to metaphor (*Str.* 5. 21. 4) and to symbols (5. 89. 2). Origen, too, speaks often of the need for allegorizing narratives from Old and New Testaments (*Ioh.* 33. 24; 201. 27; 267. 1; 337. 31; 376. 11; 445. 9), and relying on Gal. 4. 24 says that the whole story of Abraham is an allegory (339. 15). In his treatise *De principiis* he prefers to use the term *anagōgē* (which we shall presently discuss), and relates it to *allegoria* in *Ioh.* 33. 24; 111. 7; 201. 27; and 240. 32. His position is not quite clear, since in a fragment on Luke (254 XLVI) he criticizes Marcionite rejection of allegory, while in *Ioh.* he says that the heterodox rejoice in allegories and refer a story about healings to therapies of the soul (352. 14).

The word remained popular among Greek allegorizers, e.g., in Porphyry, *De antro nympharum*, pp. 56. 8 and 57. 20, Nauck ed. 2, and in later Neoplatonists. Because of its late origin the word does not occur in the Septuagint, and Christians often hesitated to use it. A third-century Egyptian named Nepos wrote an *Elenchos allegoristōn*, and the school of Antioch vigorously resisted Alexandrian usage (cf. H. N. Bate in *Journal of Theological Studies* 24, 1922–3, 59–66).

3. amphibolia

It is worth noting that allegorizers claim that passages they can explain are *not* ambiguous. Heraclitus says that Homer does not use ambiguous or recherché (*zétoumenais*) allegories; he delivered a clear method of interpretation to us (8. 9). Similarly Justin argues against Trypho that prophetic expressions are not ambiguous (*Dial.* 51. 1, 2).

4. anagōgē

This word is usually employed in the sense of a "reference" to first principles (cf. Liddell-Scott-Jones, *Lexicon*, s.v.). Thus Cornutus speaks of "referring" the twelve labours to Heracles (64. 15) and mythical traditions to the elements of nature (76. 1). In both instances the process is directed from the form of the story to its ultimate content. Justin's direction is the opposite (*Dial.* 56. 16); he "refers" things to the scriptures.

Clement says that the Lord used parables to lead (*anagein*) men from one world to another (*Str.* 6. 126. 3). This is not the technical exegetical use, but comes close to it; it is paralleled by the Neoplatonic use of *anagōgē* for the lifting up of the soul to God (Liddell-Scott-Jones, citing Porphyry, *Sent.* 30; Iamblichus, *De myst.* 3. 7; cf. Stephanus-Dindorf I, 339, ed. 2).

In Origen it is a technical term of exegesis. He first uses it in his *Commentary on the Psalms* (Lomm. 11. 425) and in that on Lamentations (245, Klostermann), where he speaks of "the laws of *anagōgē*", obviously the equivalent of Philo's "laws of allegory". The word recurs in *Princ.* 330. 2; 333. 6, 13, 26 ("mystical *anagōgē*", 333. 6); and it is frequent in the *Commentary on John*. In *Contra Celsum* 4. 21 it is contrasted with *historia*. It is thus Origen's substitute for "allegory" (although he can use either word), and emphasizes the spiritual nature and purpose of his exegesis. It hints that a deeper meaning lies within the written word. On its use by Origen cf. S. Läuchli in *Theologische Zeitschrift* 10 (1954), 175–97.

5. apomnémoneumata

This is the title given by Justin (*Apol.* 1. 66. 3; cf. 33. 5 and *Dial.* 100–7) to the gospels. Such works are defined by rhetoricians (cited in Moulton-Milligan, *Vocab.* 67) as fairly extensive accounts of someone's words and/or deeds. The verb is used by Papias to describe the work of the evangelist Mark, who recorded the tradition delivered him by Peter (Eusebius, *H.E.* 3. 39. 15). We have already discussed (pp. 62, 77) the historical emphasis of Papias. This recurs even among allegorizers. Thus Clement (*Str.* 5. 82. 4) uses the verb of Luke's description of Paul at Athens, and Origen uses it in regard to the historical accuracy of the gospels (*Ioh.* 143. 29; 173. 22).

6. *deigma, hypodeigma*

Deigma is used by Philo in discussing the story of the serpent in Eden (*Opif.* 157). Such things as speaking serpents are not mythical fictions but *deigmata* (examples) of "types" (i.e., typical examples) which encourage allegory in accordance with data given through hidden meanings. The word recurs in Jude 7 (a warning example), and it passed into Hebrew as a loan-word meaning *mashal* or parable; cf. I. Heinemann, *Altjüdische Allegoristik* (Breslau, 1935), 17. It is employed by Theophilus as the equivalent of "Prefiguration" of a cosmic or eschatological secret (*Ad Autol.* 2. 14–16). Since his exegesis is largely Jewish, we may suspect that his usage of this word is Jewish too.

Writers who use better Greek employ *hypodeigma* (2 Peter 2. 6 uses it to replace Jude's *deigma*). We find it in Heb. 4. 11 (instance), 8. 5, and 9. 23 (pattern). It is frequent in 1 Clement, where it means pattern or example (occasionally *hypogrammos*). Papias speaks of Judas as a great *hypodeigma* of impiety in this world (cf. 2 Peter).

In Christian usage both words often have an eschatological meaning, but this comes from the context rather than from the word itself.

7. *dianoia, noein, hyponoia*

True "understanding" of the poets or of scripture is characteristic of allegorizers. Heraclitus contrasts "what is meant" (*to nooumenon*) with "what is said" (8. 18) and speaks of allegorical understanding of things which are (really) meant (26. 4). Hermes, the Logos, is the one who interprets everything which is meant (94. 16). The same term is used by Clement and Origen, as well as by the gnostic allegorizer Heracleon, who contrasts it with the "simple" sense (fr. 18 Völker); cf. J. Mouson in *Eph. theol. Lov.* 30 (1954), 315–20.

Related to this is the "understanding" (*dianoia*) of the allegorizers (though Heraclitus does not use the word in this sense). Philo uses the word to refer to "an instrument for knowing God and celestial matters, celestial wisdom and ecstasy" (H. Leisegang, Index to Cohn-Wendland's Philo, VII, 182). This last use—understanding of ecstasy—is exactly paralleled in Cornutus (47. 22). The word also has a more specifically exegetical meaning. Philo (*Praem.* 61) speaks of the literal meaning as "a symbol of invisible understanding (*dianoia*)". And Cornutus (62. 18, 19) says of a myth that it has a "manifest understanding".

These last two examples show how close *dianoia* comes to *hyponoia*, the word used from Plato's time for the content to be understood by the understanding. Philo frequently uses *hyponoia* in relation to allegory; *hyponoia* means *physiologia* ("allegorical meaning") in *Somn.* 1. 120, and in *Praem.* 65 he speaks of allegories *kath' hyponoian*. On the other hand, Heraclitus does not use the word, and Cornutus usually uses the verb *hyponoein* in its ordinary meaning "to suppose", though sometimes verb and noun are related to allegorical meanings (32. 1; 45. 6; 74. 3). As we have already observed (p. 122), Plutarch says that the Platonic *hyponoia* is the equivalent of *allegoria*. Clement (*Quis dives* 26. 1; *Str.* 5. 24. 1) and Porphyry (*De Styge* in Stob. *Ecl.* 2. 1. 19) use it in the same way. Origen apparently prefers not to use it.

8. emphainein

This word, meaning "to make plain" or "to make manifest" the true meaning of an allegory, is found nineteen times in Cornutus but not in Heraclitus or in early Christian writers (in this sense). Cornutus speaks of an "understanding" as "manifest" (62. 18, 19). Clement uses it of the meaning, now manifest, of a prefiguration or allegory (frequent in *Paed.* and elsewhere). For Origen the coming of Jesus brought the law and the prophets *eis toumphanes* that they were written by heavenly grace (*Princ.* 4. 1. 7; cf. *Ioh.* 119. 18, etc.).

9. exégésis

The noun and the verb ordinarily refer simply to "telling", "recounting", or "narrating" something. The sense of "exegesis" seems to originate in the first century B.C., in writers like Diodorus and Dionysius of Halicarnassus (Liddell-Scott-Jones, *Lexicon*, s.v.). Philo speaks of exegeses of the sacred writings as taking place through allegorical meanings (*hyponoiai*) expressed in allegories (*Vit. cont.* 78) and refers to the exegete of the sacred writings (*Spec.* 1. 159). He uses these words very rarely, however. In Heraclitus the verb means "explain" (46. 10). Cornutus uses the noun in reference to his own explanation of Hesiod's *Theogony* as partly tradition and partly mythical additions (31. 13).

In 1 Clement the word is used of narratives (49. 2; 50. 1). Hermas has the same usage (*Vis.* 4. 2. 5) but also uses the word in relation to explanatory exegesis of a parabolic tower (*Vis.* 3. 7. 4). Papias wrote five books of *Exegeses of Dominical Oracles*—obviously exegetical.

Justin frequently uses both noun and verb, although they often mean "translation" or "translate" (e.g., *Dial.* 124. 3). Theophilus tells us that no human being can properly set forth the *exégésis* and the whole divine plan of the work of creation (*Ad Autol.* 2. 12). Here the word may mean either "account" or "exegesis". But since he is contrasting the poets with the Spirit-inspired Moses, we should probably translate "account".

Some gnostics, such as Basilides (Clement, *Str.* 4. 81. 1) and his son Isidore (ibid., 6. 53. 2), wrote *exégétika*, and Origen refers to his own *Commentary on John* in the same way (*Ioh.* 226. 5, etc.). Like Papias, Clement (*Quis dives* 3. 1) speaks of *exégésis* of the oracles of the Lord, and uses verb and noun to refer primarily to explanations, e.g., *Paed.* 2. 84. 1: "explanation of symbolic statements".

10. *epilusis*

This word seems to be a product of the second century A.D. Sextus Empiricus uses it of the "solution" of sophistical arguments (*Pyrrh. hyp.* 2. 246); Vettius Valens, for "solutions" or "explanations" (221. 9; 330. 10 Kroll); Heliodorus, for "explanations" of dreams (cf. W. Bauer, *Wörterbuch zum Neuen Testament,* ed. 4, s.v.)

It does not seem to occur in any writer before Hermas, who uses it six times of the "explanation" of parables; cf. Mark 4. 34, "privately he explained (*epeluen*) everything to his own disciples". In 2 Peter 1. 20 we read that "every prophecy of scripture does not take place with private (or, its own) *epilusis*": cf. Mark 4. 11, "to those outside, everything takes place in parables". What does 2 Peter have in mind? Clement (*Paed.* 2. 14. 2) may provide an example of what 2 Peter is criticizing; he says that the coin of Matt. 17. 27 may well have "further unknown explanations", which he will not now discuss. Perhaps 2 Peter means that "not every prophecy has a special, secret solution" —or that "no prophecy has a private, secret solution". The word was used by the gnostic Heracleon (Origen, *Ioh.* 148. 12).

On the partial parallels to 2 Peter in Philo, cf. R. Knopf, *Die Briefe Petri et Judä* (Göttingen, 1912), 283–4, and J. B. Mayor, *The Epistle of St Jude and the Second Epistle of St Peter* (London, 1907), 111–13.

11. *herméneia*

In Philo the verb *herméneuein* usually means to "translate" from Hebrew to Greek (H. Leisegang, Index to Cohn-Wendland's Philo VII, 297), and this usage of the verb and related words continues in early Christianity. Paul speaks of the "translation of languages(?)" in 1 Cor. 12. 10 and 14. 26 (cf. 14. 27, 28). Probably in the same sense Papias (Eusebius, *H.E.* 3. 39. 15) calls Mark the "translator" of Peter, for he also says that "each translated the *logia* of Matthew as he was able" (ibid., 16). Justin (*Dial.* 103. 5) and Tatian (*Or.* 1. 3) also use the word of translations. For its use in relation to the Septuagint cf. Irenaeus, *Adv. haer.* 3. 21. 2; Clement, *Str.* 1, 148–9.

On the other hand, it also means "interpretation" in an exegetical sense. Philo distinguishes prophecy from interpretation (*Mos.* 2. 191; cf. H. A. Wolfson, *Philo*, Cambridge, 1947, II, 42), and Papias refers to the "interpretations" of the elders (Eusebius, *H.E.* 3. 39. 3). Justin (*Dial.* 124. 4) and Melito of Sardis (*Hom.* 41, 42) refer to the "interpretation" of a psalm or parable, while Tatian refers to divine revelations as "interpretations" (*Or.* 12. 3).

In the Greek world allegorization is a "trope of interpretation" (Heraclitus 8. 12); Heraclitus (though not Cornutus) relates interpretation to the reason personified in Hermes (*hermeneia*; 43. 10, 11; 77. 10; 80. 18; 94. 17). This etymology is also reported by the Christian apologists Aristides (10. 3) and Justin (*Apol.* 1. 21. 2). Clement of Alexandria speaks of allegorization as "mystical interpretation" (*Str.* 5. 37. 1).

Thus when Ignatius of Antioch tells Christians to avoid those who interpret Judaism to them (*Philad.* 6. 1) he may well have Old Testament exegesis in mind.

Origen uses the word once in *Princ.*, more often in the *Commentary on John*. Here it usually refers to the translation of Hebrew names into Greek (e.g., 218. 14)—a translation which itself results, as in Philo, in symbolic interpretation. Origen also refers to the "interpretation" of John by Heracleon (180. 27; 181. 32).

12. *theologia*

This word has been thoroughly discussed by F. Kattenbusch, "Zur Geschichte der Ausdrücke *theologia, theologein, theologos*", *Zeitschrift für Theologie und Kirche* N.F. 11 (1930), 161–205, and by A. J. Festugière, *La révélation d'Hermès Trismégiste* II (Paris, 1949), 598–605. We need to consider only its relation to allegorization. The verb is not uncommon in Heraclitus (six times; *ektheologein* once, with the same meaning), who uses it in regard to the content of allegorical language, though he does not use the noun. The noun, but not the verb, occurs twice in Cornutus, where it refers to the "ancient theology", the content of the poets which must be separated from their mythical additions (31. 17; 63. 13). Philo uses the verb once (*Opif.* 12) in speaking of the work of Moses, whom he calls the *theologos* (*Mos.* 2. 115; *Praem.* 53). Apparently he does not use *theologia*.

The first Christian writer to use the word is Justin, who uses the verb to mean "to call someone God" (*Dial.* 56. 15; cf. *kyriolegein* in *Dial.* 56. 14, 15) and "to allegorize" in *Dial.* 113. 2 (cf. Kattenbusch, op. cit., 198).

13. *theōria*

Philo uses the noun in speaking of the allegorical content of a passage. One can understand allegorically the *theōrian tén dia symbolōn* (*Spec.* 2. 29). Heraclitus comes close to this expression when he says of a story that it has a *physiké theōria* of allegory (39. 16). He uses the word nine times in this sense. Cornutus, on the other hand, ordinarily uses the verb *theōrein* simply to mean "observe" (six times), though he employs the noun once in reference to allegorical content (23. 8).

In Origen, *Contra Celsum* 2. 6, we find *mystiké theōria* contrasted with the letter. Later on, the word became important in the conflict between Antioch and Alexandria. Cf. A. Vaccari in *Biblica* 1 (1920), 3 ff.; H. N. Bate in *Journal of Theological Studies* 24 (1922–3), 59 ff.

14. *ménuein*

This verb seems to be a little weaker than *ainissesthai*, but it conveys a similar meaning for the "hinting" or "indicating" on which allegorization is supposed to be based. Philo uses it to describe the allegorical method of the holy scriptures (*Opif.* 77), their use of symbols (*Mos.* 1. 217; 2. 228), and of allegories (*Dec.* 101). It is frequent in Justin and the Valentinians used it to refer to the hidden significance of scripture (Irenaeus, *Adv. haer.* 1. 3. 1). So also Clement, *Paed.* 2. 43.3; 110. 2; *Str.* 1. 32. 3, etc.; Origen, *Princ.* 324. 4, etc. (though in *Ioh.* 424 it means only "indicate" without an allegorical allusion).

15. *mystérion, mystikos,* etc.

Three thorough essays deal with the early patristic use of this word: H. v. Soden, "*mystérion* und Sacramentum in den zwei ersten Jahrhunderten der Kirche", *Zeitschrift für die neutestamentliche Wissenschaft* 12 (1911), 188–227; K. Prümm, " 'Mysterion' von Paulus bis Origenes", *Zeitschrift für katholische Theologie* 61 (1937), 391–425; and A. D. Nock, "Hellenistic Mysteries and Christian Sacraments", *Mnemosyne* IV 5 (1952), 177–213, especially 188–92 and 204–10. For Philo cf. P. Ziegert in *Theologische Studien und Kritiken* 76 (1894), 706–32; for Clement, H. G. Marsh in *Journal of Theological Studies* 37 (1936), 64–80; for Origen, H. von Balthasar in *Recherches de science religieuse* 26 (1936), 513–62; 27 (1937), 38–64. On *mystérion* in Greek philosophy generally, H. Leisegang in *Philologische Wochenschrift* 52 (1932), 1189–96.

We do not intend to review this material, but to deal only with the question whether the terminology necessarily implies religious concerns. It is sometimes held that (*a*) allegorical interpretation was a feature of mystery religions, and/or (*b*) that Philo's Judaism or the Alexandrians' Christianity came close to the mystery religions because of this terminology. (On Philo cf. H. A. Wolfson, *Philo*, Cambridge, 1947, I, 24, 25 and 44–55.)

There is no special mystery influence in Chrysippus' reference to Stoic theology as "divine rites" (*SVF* II, 42, 1008; *teletai* because "last" to be taught in the curriculum, *teleutaioi*). Then when Heraclitus uses similar language in dealing with Homer, we should not expect more than "literary religion" or "religiosity". He calls the poet "the great hierophant of heaven and the gods" (100. 9; cf. 85. 8) and speaks of initiation into the mystic wisdom of the Homeric rites (75. 18). The allegorical method leads to the "divine rites of Homer" (85. 8). This seems to be no more than traditional Stoic language, even though he says that the identification of Apollo with the sun is plain "from the mystic discourses of the theology of the ineffable rites" (10. 8). These discourses may be no more than the poems of Homer allegorically interpreted. Philo and Clement use the same language in referring to the allegorical meaning of scripture. There is no evidence that the mysteries are in any way related to cultus.

Furthermore, there is no evidence for the existence of allegorical exegesis as such in the mystery religions, even though like all religions they used symbols. The only evidence we possess comes from the fourth-century *Confession of Cyprian* (cf. M. P. Nilsson in *Harvard Theological Review* 40, 1947, 167–76), and cannot be used to portray the earlier situation. Certainly ritual books were used in the mysteries, but allegorical explanations seem to have been purely personal, as in the case of Plutarch's treatise *On Isis and Osiris* and Porphyry's explanation of Mithraic doctrine in his work *On the Cave of the Nymphs*. It may be relevant that Philo's own allegorizations, hardly "canonical", were preserved by Christians rather than Jews. In other words, the "mystery-language" of allegorizers has no more cultic significance than Galen's references to the study of nature as the truest mystery (*De usu partium* 7. 14 and 12. 6), superior to the rites of Eleusis and Samothrace (17. 1).

Within Christianity the notion of the content of allegory as a mystery first occurs in Mark 4. 11 (cf. 4. 33, 34); it means "a secret" like the "secrets of God" in the prophets, known only to the Dead Sea commentators on Habakkuk. The secret or mystery is the eschatological, *heilsgeschichtlich* understanding of Jesus' words (Mark) or of the Old Testament prophecies and prefigurations (Paul, twenty-one times). It is the fulfilment of the prophecies, hidden from hostile powers (Paul; Ignatius, *Eph.* 19. 1; *Magn.* 9. 2; *Trall.* 2. 3). In Justin too, it refers to the secret content of the Old Testament, known only to Christians who have the spiritual gift of exegesis (cf. E. Hatch, *Essays in Biblical Greek*, London, 1890, 60; von Soden, op. cit., 201–3).

The Valentinians used the noun, the adjective *mystikos*, and the adverb *mystikōs* in the same way. As we have already seen (p. 68) they held that the Saviour taught, in part, figuratively and mystically (*Exc. Theod.* 66). The Carpocratians, giving exegesis of Mark 4. 11 ff., said that Jesus "spoke in a mystery, privately to his disciples and apostles" (Irenaeus, *Adv. haer.* 1. 25. 4). Relying on the same New Testament passage, Valentinians held that the Saviour gave hints, mysteriously, through parables (ibid., 1. 3. 1).

Even the more literal-minded Theophilus uses *mystérion* twice (*Ad Autol.* 2. 15, 28) and "mysteriously" once (2. 26) in reference to the secrets of God underlying the letter of scripture.

All the emphasis of this word is laid on the secrecy involved. It implies that outsiders cannot understand one's exegesis. It has nothing to do with pagan religious rites.

16. *oikonomia*

Like *theologia*, this word refers to the content of the revelation as understood by the allegorical method or something similar. It is used of the "dispensation" of God, his plan of salvation which he is working out. It need not have any eschatological connotation; Philo (*Dec.* 53) says that God "always dispenses everything savingly". In Pauline thought, however, there is a strong emphasis on eschatology, and the word is therefore used to refer to the divine arrangement of the history of salvation, the "dispensation of the mystery" (Eph. 3. 9; cf. 1. 10).

In Justin's *Dialogue* it is used chiefly in regard to Christ's incarnation, birth, human life, and passion (30. 3; 31. 1; 45. 4; 67. 6; 87. 5; 120. 1). These are *oikonomiai* "according to the will of the Father" (103. 3), instances of the work of God. The story of Jonah also contains an *oikonomia*, for it is a prophecy of Christ (107. 3). And in the lives of the patriarchs are some *oikonomiai* of great mysteries (134. 2). In their (clearly allegorical) polygamous marriages, "a certain *oikonomia*, and all mysteries, was performed through them" (141. 4). As in Ephesians, *oikonomia* and *mystérion* are related. One sees the plan of salvation only through careful, allegorical exegesis.

For other instances cf. Melito, *Homily* 56, p. 125 Bonner; E. Schwartz, *Index Tatiani*, p. 86; and Theophilus, *Ad Autol.* 2. 12, 15. Like Justin, Origen says that the lives of the patriarchs contain "certain mystical *oikonomiai*, made plain through the divine scriptures" (*Princ.* 309. 1), as well as mysteries.

17. *homoiōmas, homoiōsis, parabolé, paroimia*

Perhaps because of theological concern with *homoiōsis* in Gen. 1. 26, 27, perhaps because of concern with *parabolé* in the tradition, Christian writers are not fond of *homoiōma* or *homoiōsis*, as used in reference to literary form. The first occurs in Theophilus, *Ad Autol.* 2. 12, the second in Justin, *Dial.* 77. 4: the Holy Spirit often speaks in parables and similitudes.

The word preferred is *parabolé*. According to Quintilian it is not the same as a similitude but contains it; it is a longer similitude (*Inst.* 5. 11. 23). In every parable either the similitude precedes the matter itself, or the matter precedes the similitude (8. 3. 77). Philo (*Conf.* 99) uses the word of mean "comparison", but it does not occur in Heraclitus or Cornutus.

In the New Testament the parable is treated as a means of concealing and revealing at the same time; thus it comes close to enigma or allegory. In Mark Jesus uses parables in his enigmatic preaching to priests, scribes, and elders (3. 23; 12. 1, 12), though they can understand the point at times (12. 12). He also uses them for private teaching to his disciples and sometimes gives private explanations (chap. 4, eight times). In Mark 7. 17 a general statement is treated as a parable and given a private explanation. In Mark 13. 28, however, *parabolé* means simply "comparison". The same two uses are found in Matthew and Luke. Matthew explains Jesus' use of parables by citing Psalm 77 (78). 2: "I will open my mouth in parables; I will emit things hidden from the time of creation." In Heb. 9. 9 the word has the sense of "prefiguration" or "example", as in 11. 19.

It is frequent in Hermas, who has a whole book of parables of his own ("similitudes", Latin). They have to be explained by an angel. Barnabas speaks of the Old Testament "land of milk and honey" as "a parable of the Lord" (i.e., prefiguration), understood only by the man who possesses wisdom and understanding of the Lord's secrets (6. 10). He holds that the Old Testament predictions of present and future lie (hidden) in parables (17. 2; cf. Justin [?] in Irenaeus, *Adv. haer.* 5. 26. 2; p. 122 above).

In Justin, too, parable is equivalent to prefiguration. The prophets use parables or mysteries or symbolic actions (*Dial.* 68. 6); they use parables and prefigurations (90. 2). Among the Old Testament parables are the prefigurations of Christ (36. 2; 52. 1; 97. 3; 113. 6; 114. 2; 115. 1; 123. 8) and the reference to "the blood of the grape" (63. 2). The demonic power is called Samaria "in a parable" (78. 10). Justin associates parable with mystery (97. 3; 115. 1), thus perhaps reflecting Mark's insistence on the mystery-character (secrecy) of parables. When he says that "in a parable" Christ is called a stone, and "in tropology" (see below), Jacob and Israel (114. 2), there is no real difference between the terms.

Melito of Sardis also treats parable as prefiguration. "That which was spoken through the parable was illuminated by fulfilment" (*Homily* 35; cf. 40–2). Similarly the *Preaching of Peter* says that the prophets spoke partly through parables, partly through enigmas, and partly straightforwardly and explicitly (Clement, *Str.* 6. 128. 1). There is no real difference between parable and enigma (cf. *Exc. Theod.* 66), any more than there is between parable and allegory in Clement of . Alexandria (cf. *Str.* 6. 126. 3 and 127. 1, cited by W. Völker, *Der wahre Gnostiker nach Clemens Alexandrinus*, Berlin–Leipzig, 1952, 362–3). The definitions which he and Origen provide for "parable" (cf. E. Klostermann in *Zeitschrift für die neutestamentliche Wissenschaft* 37, 1938, 61) come from grammarians and rhetoricians, and imply that parables are allegories. In Origen's *Commentary on John* he generally reserves the word for the parables of the gospels, but it also means "allegory" (415. 8); he too associates it with "mystery" (259. 31).

When the gnostics treated parables as allegories, therefore, they were not innovating but following the tradition of Christians, grammarians, and rhetoricians.

Another word for parable or similitude is *paroimia*, found in John 10. 6; 16. 25, 29 (John does not use *parabolé*). This usage is that of Sirach 39. 3: "the hidden aspects of *paroimiai*" (cf. 47. 17). Sometimes, as in 2 Peter 2. 22 and Athenagoras, *Leg.* 34, 1, the word means simply "proverb" (as in the Greek title of the Book of Proverbs).

All this terminology is fluid. Clement of Alexandria (*Str.* 6. 130. 1) says that *paroimia* = *parabolé* = *ainigma*. Similar fluidity is found in the Hebrew *māshāl*; cf. A. R. Johnson in *Vetus Testamentum* Suppl. III (1955), 162–9.

18. *pneumatikōs*

The earliest Christian use of this word, meaning "allegorically", is found in the Apocalypse of John (11. 9), where "allegorically" Jerusalem is called Egypt and Sodom (in the Old Testament). A hint of such a meaning is given by Paul in 1 Cor. 2. 14, where he argues that spiritual matters are spiritually discerned, and only by the *pneumatikos*.

Another example occurs in 1 Clement 47. 3, where the author says that "in truth, Paul wrote to you *pneumatikōs* about himself, Cephas, and Apollos". The word must mean "allegorically", since it is Clement's substitute for *meteschématisa* in 1 Cor. 4. 6—a word which refers to a trope like allegory (cf. F. H. Colson in *Journal of Theological Studies* 17, 1915–16, 379–84).

The word became a favourite among the Valentinians and in Clement and Origen. Especially at Alexandria it was regarded as a better word than "allegorically", since it pointed more clearly towards the inspiration of content and exegesis and away from literary form (cf. H. de Lubac, *Histoire et Esprit*, Paris, 1950, 141).

19. *sémainein*

This is another of the words which point towards the underlying allegorical content of a work being interpreted; it is practically equivalent to *ainissesthai* or *ménuein*, but suggests that the allegory is fairly evident to the reader.

It occurs three times in the Gospel of John (12. 33; 18. 32; 21. 19), and in commenting on the first instance W. Bauer notes that it is a "terminus technicus für die nur andeutende Rede des Orakelspenders". He cites Josephus, *Ant.* 7. 214 and 10. 241, as well as a fragment of the philosopher Heraclitus: the Delphic oracle neither speaks (plainly) not conceals, but "indicates" (Plutarch, *Pyth. orac.* 404 e). For this reason it is especially appropriate in relation to allegorization. Heraclitus (the exegete) uses it in his definition of allegory (5. 16): "It says one thing and signifies another." He uses the word seven more times in this sense, though he has a slight preference for *hyposémainein* (ten times), since the prefix *hypo* further stresses the hiddenness of the meaning. Cornutus, on the other hand, uses *sémainein* only once. Among later allegorizers it is commonly used. The gnostic Heracleon employs it three times. Capernaum signifies the "ends of the earth" (fr. 11 Völker); the Jewish passover signifies the passion of the Saviour (fr. 12); and Jesus' journey from Capernaum to Jerusalem signifies the transition from the material to the psychic realm (fr. 13). It is very frequently used by Clement and Origen, and Porphry uses it at least twice (*De antro nympharum* 32, p. 78, 17 Nauck ed. 2; *De Styge* in Stob. *Ecl.* 2. 1. 19).

20. *symbolon*

Among the many meanings of *symbolon* there is the semi-technical allegorical usage, according to which the word refers to both form and content of allegorical speech: symbols are things spoken allegorically (Demetrius, *Eloc.* 243). The earliest example comes from Chrysippus, who describes some person as saying that Athena's birth from the head of Zeus is a *symbolon* that the ruling principle is in the head (*SVF* II 908, cf. 909). The word is very common in Philo and seems to be his favourite term for allegory. "Most of the statements made in the laws (of Moses) are manifest symbols of things unseen, and expressions of what is not expressed" (*Spec.* 3. 178; cf. *Jos.* 28). The word occurs especially in relation to names and objects, though names and objects are not clearly distinguished.

Heraclitus says that Homer theologizes and allegorizes by portraying things through symbols (37. 7). To use symbols is to speak metaphorically (96. 12). Since all these terms can be equated, it is not surprising that Heraclitus stresses Homer's symbolic speech (41. 5; 86. 15; 98. 2).

Cornutus speaks seven times of things or their properties as "symbols", and once combines "symbol" with "enigma" (76. 4).

Justin is the first Christian to use the word, in referring to objects in the Old Testament which had a prefigurative meaning for Christians (or an allegorical one). It occurs six times in the *First Apology* and fifteen times in the *Dialogue*. In *Dial.* 42. 4 (cf. 111. 1) he associates prefigurations, symbols, and proclamations.

It is very common in Clement, partly because of the influence of

Philo. Cf. C. Mondésert, *Clément d'Alexandrie* (Paris, 1944), 88; also in *Recherches de science religieuse* 26 (1936), 158–80. Origen uses it fairly frequently in his *Commentary on John* in reference to actions, persons, and places. The presence of a *symbolon* suggests the use of *anagōgé* (545. 18).

21. *tropologia*

This is not a common allegorizing term, but it is interesting to see how its meaning changes from Justin to Origen. For Justin it means "analogy" or "comparison" (*Dial.* 57. 2); he equates it with "parable" in *Dial.* 114. 2. And when he rejects a Jewish analogy in *Dial.* 129. 2, he calls it a *tropologia* of "sophists" (Jewish teachers).

In Origen it is used, like parable, to mean "allegory". The verb *tropologein* means both to compare (probably so in *C. Cels.* 4. 51) and to take allegorically (*Ioh.* 439. 13). In *Matt. comm.* 10. 14, p. 17, the "mere letter" is contrasted with *tropologein*, which involves *anagōgé*.

22. *typos*

On this word perhaps the most important discussions are those by L. Goppelt, *Typos* (Gütersloh, 1939); R. Bultmann, "Ursprung und Sinn der Typologie als hermeneutischer Methode", *Theologische Literaturzeitung* 75 (1950), 205–12; and Erich Auerbach, *Mimesis* (Princeton, 1953), 16, 48–9, 73–6.

Bultmann has tried to provide a theological ground for his own rejection of "typology" by arguing that it rests on a cyclical notion of history, as compared with the fulfilment of prophecy, which does not. In our opinion such distinctions cannot be validated. Actually "typology" is only one form of allegorization, and like allegorization in general must be avoided when one seeks for the author's original intention.

Further distinctions must be made. *Typos* can mean:

1. "Model" or "example" to be imitated or heeded, as in 1 Cor. 10. 6, 11. On these verses Johannes Weiss comments, "Here *typos* does not have the special meaning of prophetic prefiguration; it has the more general sense of example or model, in this case a warning" (*Komm.* on 1 Cor., 252, 254 n. 1). This sense is also found in 1 Thess. 1. 7; 2 Thess. 3. 9; Phil. 3. 17; 1 Tim. 4. 12; Titus 2. 7; and 1 Peter 5. 3. It is the equivalent of *hypodeigma* in 1 Clement.

2. It can also mean "prototype" or "model", as in Ex. 25. 40; in this

context the plural can refer to heavenly archetypes as in Philo, *Opif.* 157 (examples of *typoi*, encouraging one to allegory), and in Heb. 8. 5. 3. Then there is what is sometimes regarded as the specifically Christian, eschatological sense, in which the earlier events of the *Heilsgeschichte* roughly correspond with the later ones. This is found in Rom. 5. 14, where Adam is regarded as a *typos* (prefiguration) of the one to come (cf. 1 Cor. 15. 45–7). The background of such ideas lies in contemporary Judaism, where the new age of the future was described in terms borrowed from the golden age or ages of the past.

The word *typos* in this third sense is rare in the New Testament. Corresponding to it is "antitype"; thus in an eschatological context 1 Peter 3. 21 compares the salvation of Noah with its Christian *antitypos*, baptism. In a semi-Platonic context we find "model" and "copy" in Heb. 9. 24; and in a semi-gnostic context we find flesh the *antitypos* of spirit in 2 Clement 14. 3. It is the context which determines the meaning. In Athenagoras, *Leg.* 17. 2, *typos* is a sculptor's model; and Melito (*Hom.* 41–6) combines sculpture with eschatology by arguing that when the statue is completed the model is of no value. The fluidity of the terminology can be seen from *Hom.* 38. *Typos* = *eikōn* = *paradeigma*.

What might be considered the "technical" use of *typos* in the third sense listed above is found in the Epistle of Barnabas. The sacrificed goat is a prefiguration of Jesus (chap. 7; also called *homoiotés*, 7. 10); the sacrificial wood is a prefiguration of the cross (8. 1); and various actions of Moses are prefigurations of Jesus (chap. 12). What Barnabas is doing is seeking allegorical meanings in every jot and tittle of the Old Testament. The fact that only the three examples listed above are called *typoi* does not prove that Barnabas reserved the word for them. For as we have seen so far the existence of a technical meaning for *typos* has yet to be proved.

For Justin, *typoi* are generally things or events, as compared with sayings. The prophets concealed the truth in parables and in prefigurations (*Dial.* 90. 2). *Typoi* are mysteries (91. 3; 111. 2); they took place symbolically (111. 1). Justin associates prefigurations with mysteries, prefigurations with symbols (42. 4; 111. 1), and symbols with mysteries (138. 1). These prefigurations were caused by the Holy Spirit (114. 1).

The Valentinians also emphasized *typoi*. Like more orthodox writers (as we shall see) they did not trouble to differentiate the second from the third meaning of *typos*. In other words, they confused celestial geography with history. In their view everything on earth is a *typos* of something in the heavens (Irenaeus, *Adv. haer.* 1. 7. 2). In Ptolemaeus' letter to Flora he states that the law was *typikon kai symbolikon*. The Saviour translated it from its perceptible sense to one spiritual and invisible. The law contained images and symbols which have now become spiritual (thus *typos* probably is the equivalent of image, *eikōn*, as in Melito's *Homily*). Another Valentinian, Heracleon, taught that the Passover was a prefiguration of the passion (fr. 12 Völker); the wood of the whip he used in the temple was a prefiguration of the cross (fr. 13). Theodotus held that the Saviour taught *typikōs* and mystically (*Exc.* 66); examples occur in *Exc.* 23. 2 and 33. 3.

There is no difference between this terminology and that, for example, of Irenaeus. The difference lies entirely in theological presuppositions, not in exegetical methods. Irenaeus (*Adv. haer.* 4. 30. 4) tells of a presbyter who urged him *typum quaerere*, and added that *nihil otiosum est eorum quaecumque inaccusabilia posita sunt in scripturis*. The Valentinians could easily have agreed. Both Irenaeus (2. 23. 1) and Hippolytus (*Dan. comm.* 4. 23. 5; 4. 30. 9) associate *typos* and *eikōn*, and while they themselves lay emphasis on historical prefiguration, such an emphasis is not implied by their terminology.

Clement's *typoi* come largely from the Old Testament, though at times he uses the word to mean "example" or "archetypal form." He combines *typos* with allegory (*Str.* 2. 20. 2) and with mystery (*De Pascha* fr. 28). Origen usually uses the word in relation to the Old Testament; in *Princ.* 4. 2. 2 he criticizes a simple "typology" which lacks a foundation of philosophical theology.

The word *typos*, then, has nothing specifically Christian about it, and the modern "typological method" is not necessarily implied by the word. It is the context which gives the word its meaning.

23. *physiologia*

Since one of the main purposes of allegorization in antiquity was to discover the poet's or prophet's teaching about Nature, the word *physiologia* often means the allegorical content of the writing. Indeed, the rhetorician Menander I protested against the equation *physiologia* = *kath' hyponoian* (*Rhet. graec.* III. 138 Spengel; cited by J. Amann, *Die Zeusrede des Ailios Aristeides*, Stuttgart, 1931, 8). But the usage was common. We find it in the Stoic Diogenes of Babylon, as cited by Cicero, *De natura deorum* 1. 41; in Philo, *Somn.* 1. 120 and frequently (cf. H. Leisegang in Pauly-Wissowa-Kroll, *Real-Encyclopädie der classischen Altertumswissenschaft* XX 36–7); and in Heraclitus 94. 7 (also *physikos* thirteen times, *physikōs* eight times).

The Christian Justin (*Apol.* 1. 60. 1) speaks of creation as "that which was 'physiologized' in the *Timaeus* of Plato". He means that Plato spoke allegorically (cf. *ainissetai*, used of Plato in *Dial.* 5. 4). Clement uses *physiologia* to refer to Christian allegorical teaching. Later, however, the word acquires something of a critical note when used by less philosophical Christians against more philosophical pagans (e.g., Eusebius on Porphyry's allegorization, frequently in the third book of his *Praeparatio Evangelica*).

C. Andersen (*ZNW* 44, 1952–3, 189) takes Justin's use as more Platonic and rejects the allegorical note.

24. *Terms of reproach*

Under this heading we propose to discuss the principal terms used of those who do not accept one's exegesis. Everyone knows the term "the simpler ones" (*hoi haplousteroi*), frequent in Clement and Origen. There are other terms, however. The "unlearned" (*amatheis*) do not understand the Homeric allegories (Heraclitus 4. 8; cf. 54. 1). Such persons can also be called "sophists" (as in Justin, *Dial.* 129. 2; Clement and Origen; cf. 2 Peter 1. 16). Perhaps they interpret in a "low" manner (*tapeinōs*); cf. Justin, *Dial.* 112. 1, 4.

This is perhaps because the passages involved are *dysnoéta*, hard to understand. This word like *epilusis* does not occur before the second century. It is found in 2 Peter 3. 16 (of the Pauline epistles), in Hermas, *Sim.* 9. 14. 4 (of a parable), and in Diog. Laert. 9. 13, a "letter of Darius to Heraclitus", where the philosopher's language is regarded as *dysnoéton* and *dysexégéton*. The two terms are practically synonymous. Oracles of the false prophet Alexander are also called "hard to understand" in Lucian, *Alex.* 54.

What our opponents try to do is to try to "suit" the passages to their own theories (*harmozein*, Celsus in Origen, *C. Cels.* 4. 51; *epharmozein*, Irenaeus 1. 8. 1, of the Valentinians), or they try to "accommodate" the passages to them (*synoikeioun*, Philodemus in H. Diels, *Doxographi Graeci*, Berlin, 1879, 547 with note; *prosoikeioun*, Irenaeus, 1. 8. 2); cf. pp. 8, 23.

What they end by doing is "forcing" the passages. The word is *biazein*, already used by Dionysius of Halicarnassus (Liddell-Scott-Jones, s.v.) and found in Irenaeus 1. 3. 5 and apparently in 2. 24. 3 (*tentant violenter*); in Clement, *Str.* 3. 39. 2; 3. 61. 1; 7. 94. 4; 7. 96. 5; in Hippolytus, *Contra Noet.* 9; in Origen (frequently on John against Heracleon); and in Porphyry, *De antro nympharum* 36, p. 81 Nauck ed. 2. Plutarch (*De aud. poet.* 4. 19 f.) uses *parabiazesthai*.

This forcing can even be called "torturing" a passage, as in 2 Peter 3. 16; Irenaeus 2. 24. 2 (*impudenter extorta supputatio*; cf. Tertullian, *De anima* 18. 7); and Numenius, fr. 1 Leemans, from Eusebius, *P.E.* 14. 5 (cited by Bauer).

Three other, more technical-sounding terms can be used. We can refer to others' exegesis as "artful" (*tetechnasmené*, Justin, *Dial.* 79. 1). We can say that there is madness in the method (*methodeuein*, Philo, *Mos.* 2. 212; Polycarp, *Phil.* 7. 1, from Bauer). And we can say that others deal with a passage too easily, hence wrongly. The word *rhadiourgein* can refer to false allegorical exegesis, as in Irenaeus 1 praef. and 1. 3. 5; to mistaken textual criticism, as in Dionysius of Corinth in Eusebius, *H.E.* 4. 23. 12 (cf. Epiphanius, *Pan. haer.* 42 [Marcion]. 9. 1; 10. 4; 11. 2; 11. 6); to both of these, as in the "little labyrinth" of Hippolytus, in Eusebius, *H.E.* 5. 28. 13; or to falsity in general (Celsus in Origen, *C. Cels.* 4. 31).

25. Conclusion

Of the words we have discussed, some have reference (1) to the true content underlying the letter, others (2) to the means by which this content was concealed and revealed, others (3) to the form in which it was delivered, others (4) to the means by which the content is to be discovered, and others (5) to the result of exegesis—which is in turn the true content.

1. The content is *theologia* or *physiologia*. It was placed in the

writing by the author or by the Muses or the Spirit; it is discovered by the exegete.

2. This content was delivered in hints, suggestions and indications. One could call this method "spiritual".

3. The resulting form is *ainigma, allegoria, parabolé*. The content, is so far as it can be differentiated from the form, is *mystérion, symbolon, typos* (in various senses).

4. To understand form and content, the exegete needs to use *exégésis* and *theōria*, preferably "spiritually" and with *anagōgé*, in order to "know", to have "understanding", and to reach a solution of these mysteries. He thus shows forth and signifies the true meaning.

5. This true meaning, the same as the content mentioned above, can also be called *hyponoia*, or a recognition of the *oikonomia* underlying scripture.

It cannot be said too often that this terminology is exceedingly fluid. Moreover, Christians do not have a terminology notably different from that of their pagan contemporaries. The ultimate difference lies in the constellations of theological presuppositions, and even these are not so different at all points as one might suppose (cf. R. M. Grant, *Miracle and Natural Law in Graeco-Roman and Early Christian Thought*, Amsterdam, 1952).

Yet there are significant differences, and in our list of words there is one which could have been more significant than it was. This is *apomnémoneumata*, with its hint that the gospels are historical records, not to be reduced to symbols derived from a system wholly extraneous to them.

APPENDIX III

TEXTUAL AND LITERARY
CRITICISM

The first and most important textual and literary critic of early Christianity was Marcion. Later in the second century we encounter textual criticism among the followers of Theodotus of Byzantium; cf. H. Schöne, "Ein Einbruch der antiken Logik und Textkritik in der altchristliche Theologie", *Pisciculi F. Dölger* (Münster, 1939), 252–65; R. Walzer, *Galen on Jews and Christians* (Oxford, 1949), 75–86.

Literary criticism is also found among the anti-Montanist opponents of the gospel and apocalypse of John. Thus Epiphanius, relying on Hippolytus' work against the Roman, Gaius (cf. H. J. Lawlor and J. E. L. Oulton, *Eusebius*, II, London, 1928, 208), relates the argument that they were written not by John but by the heretic Cerinthus (*Pan haer.* 51. 3). The gospel disagrees with the other apostles, i.e., the synoptic evangelists, since they have the forty days in the desert followed by the call of the disciples (51. 4) and speak of one passover while he has two (51. 22). The angelology and eschatology of the apocalypse is ridiculous and contradicts the eschatology of Matthew (51. 32, 34; J. R. Harris, *Hermas in Arcadia*, Cambridge, 1896, 52–3). The apocalyptist is told to write to the church in Thyatira; there was no church in Thyatira (51. 33).

Origen was concerned with textual and literary questions. In Matt. 19. 19 "you shall love your neighbour as yourself" is an interpolation, since it is not found in either Mark or Luke (*Matt. comm.* 15. 14, p. 387 Klostermann), and Matthew was written first (*Matt. comm.* 1 in Eusebius, *H.E.* 6. 25. 4). He offers three explanations for the interpolation (pp. 387–8): the carelessness of scribes or boldness in emendation or additions or deletions made on the basis of personal opinion. In dealing with the mention of an eclipse (if this is what *eklipontos* means in Luke 23. 45) he says it was probably interpolated by fifth-columnists in the Church of Christ in order to make the gospels seem foolish (*Matt. comm. ser.* 134, p. 274 Klostermann). He produced his *Hexapla* by taking the Septuagint as his norm but marking with an *obelos* what was not in the Hebrew text and marking with an asterisk what he "inserted from other versions in conformity with the Hebrew" (*Matt. comm.* 15. 14, p. 388).

He regarded Hebrews as Pauline because "the ancients" said so, and because the ideas were Paul's; but only God knows who actually wrote it, since the style (*phrasis*) is more Greek than Paul's and the composition (*synthesis*) is different from his (Eusebius, *H.E.* 6. 25. 11–14).

Because of his enthusiasm for the Septuagint, however, he rejected the arguments of Julius Africanus against the authenticity of the story of Susanna (M. J. Routh, *Reliquiae sacrae*, ed. 2, Oxford, 1846, II, 225–31; W. Reichardt, *Die Briefe des Sextus Julius Africanus an Aristides und Origenes, Texte und Untersuchungen* 34, 3, Leipzig, 1909). Africanus argued that it was "modern", since the word-plays in it were possible only in Greek, it cites Ex. 23. 7 (previous prophets did not quote predecessors), and its style is different from that of Daniel. It was fictitious, since the form of revelation is different from that in the rest of Daniel, the conversations in it resemble Greek mimes, and the Jews captive in Babylon could hardly have imposed the death penalty on the wife of a friend of the king of Babylon. Africanus argued that Joachim in Susanna must have been the king's friend in Jer. 52. 32; otherwise he would not have had a large house and garden.

Finally from this period we may mention the attempt of Dionysius of Alexandria to prove that the apocalypse of John was not written by the evangelist (Eusebius, *H.E.* 7. 25; cf. J. Burel, *Denys d'Alexandrie*, Paris, 1910, 74–86; F. H. Colson, "Two Examples of Literary and Rhetorical Criticism in the Fathers", *Journal of Theological Studies* 25, 1923–4, 364–77). He uses three principal criteria: (1) the character of the author (the apocalyptist stresses his own revelation, while the evangelist does not), (2) the form of the thoughts, and (3) the general construction of the book. The last two points are again divided into threes. The different forms of thought are demonstrated by showing (1) the agreement of the gospel with the (first) epistle, (2) the complete dissimilarity of the apocalypse from both, and (3) the lack of the inter-relation between apocalypse and epistle, compared with Paul's mention of his unwritten revelations in 2 Cor. 12. 1–9. The stylistic differences are classified as (1) verbal (the apocalypse uses barbarisms), (2) logical (it uses soloecisms), and (3) syntactical (it uses vulgar phrases).

But Dionysius holds that the apocalypse is inspired (*theopneustos*) and contains wonderful hidden meanings. All he is arguing for is the necessity of taking the gospel literally and the apocalypse allegorically, since they were written by two different authors.

From these examples we see not only the existence of textual and literary criticism within the early Church, but also its relative unimportance. What mattered to the early fathers was the meaning of the traditional text, not the establishment of a true text or questions of authorship or literary form. Textual and literary criticism were ancillary to theology.

APPENDIX IV

THE *COHORTATIO* OF PSEUDO-JUSTIN

One of the most interesting ancient grammatical analyses of literal and allegorical writing is to be found in the *Cohortatio ad Graecos*, once ascribed to Justin but proved by Geffcken[1] and others to have been written after the appearance of Porphyry's work on the theology of the oracles. It begins with conventional discussions of the falsehood and inconsistency of poets and philosophers, and the superiority of divine revelation through the prophets. The principal part of the treatise, however, deals with the intimations of Christian truth to be found among Greek writers. In the author's view, as in the view of the "orientalists" discussed in our first chapter, the various Greeks he discusses had visited Egypt; there they had encountered the teachings of Moses and the other prophets. There is nothing new about the theory. The novelty lies in the way he worked it out.

"Justin" first discusses Orpheus. He literally expressed a monotheistic faith in his *Testaments* (actually a Jewish forgery), and in his *Oaths* (used by Orphics) there is an allusion to the voice of God. This voice is really the Logos.

He then inserts references to the (Jewish) *Sibylline Oracles*, which of course explicitly preach monotheism.

Then comes Homer. He was imitating Orpheus and therefore spoke mythically about a plurality of gods, "in order not to seem to disagree with Orpheus". In *Iliad.* 9. 445, however, he "plainly and openly" mentions the one God when he uses the expression "the god himself". The pronoun "himself" proves that he is referring to the real God. Another monotheistic verse is *Iliad.* 2. 204.

At this point "Justin" inserts some verses ascribed to Sophocles (actually forgeries) to show his open monotheistic teaching, and then turns to Pythagoras, who is well known to have used symbols in his teaching. Therefore we can hope only for an allegorical statement

---

[1] J. Geffcken, *Zwei griechische Apologeten* (Leipzig, 1907), 268.

about monotheism, and this we find in his doctrine of the monad. There is, however, some really monotheistic doctrine taught by Pythagoras (another forgery).

These five examples are only preliminary to the major discussion, that of Plato's borrowings from the prophets. Since God has no name, he spoke mystically to Moses, saying, "I am the existent one" (Ex. 3. 14). This doctrine was borrowed by Plato, who called God "the existent" (*Tim.* 27 d). The only difference between them is that Moses' existent is masculine in gender, Plato's neuter. Why then does Plato elsewhere use polytheistic expressions? He was afraid that he might suffer the fate of Socrates if he spoke too plainly.

Such a notion had earlier been applied to Epicurus, who was regarded as paying only lip-service to the gods and concealing his true opinions for fear of the Athenians. We first encounter it in Posidonius' treatise *On the gods* (Cicero, *De natura deorum* 1. 123; cf. 1. 85); it is also expressed by Plutarch, *Contra Epicuri beatitudinem* 21. 1102 b (H. Usener, *Epicurea*, Leipzig, 1887, p. 103, 17) as well as by the Middle Platonist Atticus (Eusebius, *Praep. ev.* 15. 5. 12) and the anti-Epicurean Christian Dionysius of Alexandria (*On nature*, in Eusebius, op. cit., 14. 27. 11 = pp. 161–2 Feltoe). Philodemus wrote his treatise *On piety* to prove Epicurus' sincerity; cf. A. J. Festugière, *Épicure et ses dieux* (Paris, 1946), 86–91.

It was among Middle Platonists that the idea was applied to Plato in order to explain why he set forth his true teaching in enigmatic form. Numenius wrote a treatise *On the things concealed by Plato* and mentioned his fear of the Areopagus (Eusebius, op. cit., 13. 5). Porphyry alludes to the same notion in his *History of philosophy* (frag. 17 Nauck) when he says that Plato spoke "enigmatically in hidden words". The basis for the notion was to be found in Plato's use of myths.

On this basis "Justin" can argue that Plato's polytheistic expressions are secondary to his monotheistic faith, even though Plato contradicts himself. He was afraid of the polytheists and for this reason ejected Homer from his ideal state. His real theology, however, expressed mystically in allegory, was derived from the prophets. After a long analysis of Plato's true doctrine and its allegorical expression, "Justin" appeals to the memory of Socrates, who wisely said that he knew

THE LETTER AND THE SPIRIT

nothing, and to that of Aristotle, who died of chagrin because of his failure to discover the cause of the currents in the Euripus channel (a late legend).[1] These men were seekers for truth. His readers should follow them and turn to the prophets.

[1] On Pseudo-Justin and Aristotle cf. L. Alfonsi in *Vigiliae Christianae* 2 (1948), 65–88.

BIBLIOGRAPHY

I. THE WISDOM OF THE ANCIENTS

ARNIM, H. VON. *Stoicorum veterum fragmenta*, I–IV, Leipzig, 1905–24.

BEVAN, E. *Sibyls and Seers*, Cambridge, Mass., 1929.

BIDEZ, J. *Vie de Porphyre*, Ghent, 1913.

BIDEZ, J. and CUMONT, F. *Les mages hellénisés*, I–II, Paris, 1938.

BOWRA, C. M. *Problems in Greek Poetry*, Oxford, 1953, 38–53.

BOYANCÉ, P. *Le culte des Muses chez les philosophes grecs*, Paris, 1937.

CORSSEN, P., "Die Schrift des Arztes Androkydes", *Rheinisches Museum* 67 (1912), 240–63.

DELATTE, A. *Les conceptions de l'enthousiasme chez les philosophes présocratiques*, Paris, 1934.

——— *Études sur la littérature pythagoricienne*, Paris, 1915, 109–36, 217–312.

DODDS, E. R. *The Greeks and the Irrational*, Berkeley, 1951.

FALTER, O. *Der Dichter und sein Gott bei den Griechen und Römern*, Würzburg, 1934.

FLACELIÈRE, R. *Plutarque sur la disparition des oracles*, Paris, 1947.

——— *Plutarque sur les oracles de la Pythie*, Paris, 1937.

HERSMAN, A. B. *Studies in Greek Allegoric Interpretation*, Chicago, 1906.

JAEGER, W. *Aristotle*, Oxford, 1934.

——— *The Theology of the Early Greek Philosophers*, Oxford, 1947.

KRANZ, W. "Das Verhältnis des Schöpfers zu seinem Werk in der althellenischen Literatur", *Neue Jahrbücher* 53 (1924), 65–86.

KROLL, W. *Studien zum Verständnis der römischen Literatur*, Stuttgart, 1924, 24–43.

LATTE, K. "Hesiods Dichterweihe", *Antike und Abendland* 2 (1946), 152–63.

LEIPOLDT, J. "Die Frühgeschichte der Lehre von der göttlichen Eingebung", *Zeitschrift für die neutestamentliche Wissenschaft* 44 (1952–3), 118–45.

LOVEJOY, A. O., and BOAS, M. *Primitivism and Related Ideas in Antiquity*, Baltimore, 1935.

MÜLLER, K. "Allegorische Dichtererklärung", Pauly-Wissowa, *Realencyclopädie der classischen Altertumswissenschaft* Suppl. IV (1924), 16–20.

NESTLE, W. "Metrodors Mythendeutung", *Philologus* 66 (1907), 503–10.

——— *Vom Mythos zum Logos*, ed. 2, Stuttgart, 1942.

NOCK, A. D. "Kornutos", Pauly-Wissowa, *Realencyclopädie* Suppl. V (1931), 995–1005.

——— *Sallustius on the Gods and the Universe*, Cambridge, 1926.

PFISTER, F. "Ekstasis", *Pisciculi F. Dölger*, Münster, 1939, 178–91.

POHLENZ, M. *Die Stoa* I–II, Göttingen, 1948.

REBESCHU, F. *L'interpretazione stoica del mito*, Castello, 1924.

REINHARDT, K. *De theologia graeca queastiones duae*, Berlin, 1910.

—— "Poseidonios", Pauly-Wissowa, *Realencyclopädie* XXII (1953), 792–805.

REPPE, R. *De L. Annaeo Cornuto*, Leipzig, 1906.

SOURY, G. *La démonologie de Plutarque*, Paris, 1942.

SPERDUTI, A. "The Divine Nature of Poetry in Antiquity", *Transactions of the American Philological Association* 81 (1950), 209–40.

TATE, J. "Allegory", *Oxford Classical Dictionary* (1949), 38–9.

—— "The Beginnings of Greek Allegory", *Classical Review* 41 (1927), 214–15.

—— "Cornutus and the Poets", *Classical Quarterly* 23 (1929), 41–5.

—— "On the History of Allegorism", *Classical Quarterly* 28 (1934), 105–14.

—— "Plato and Allegorical Interpretation", *Classical Quarterly* 23 (1929), 142–54; ibid., 24 (1930), 1–10.

—— "Socrates and the Myths", *Classical Quarterly* 27 (1933), 74–80, 159–61.

VERBEKE, G. *L'évolution de la doctrine du Pneuma*, Louvain, 1945.

VERDENIUS, W. J. "L'Ion de Platon", Mnemosyne III, 11 (1942), 233–62.

—— *Mimesis*, Leiden, 1949.

WACHSMUTH, C. *De Cratete Mallota*, Leipzig, 1860.

WASZINK, J. H. "The Proem of the Annals of Ennius", *Mnemosyne* IV, 3 (1950), 215–40.

—— and JOOSEN, J. "Allegorese", *Reallexikon für Antike und Christentum* I, (1950), 283–93.

WEHRLI, F. *Zur Geschichte der allegorischen Deutung Homers im Altertum*, Leipzig, 1928.

—— *Die Schule des Aristoteles*, Basel, 1944–.

ZIEGLER, K. "Plutarchos", Pauly-Wissowa, *Realencyclopädie* XXI (1951), 636–962.

2. MOSES, THE PROPHETS, AND THE SPIRIT

BONSIRVEN, J. *Exégèse rabbinique et exégèse paulinienne*, Paris, 1939.

BOUSSET, W. *Jüdisch-christlicher Schulbetrieb in Alexandria und Rom*, Göttingen, 1915.

BRÉHIER, E. *Les idées philosophiques et religieuses de Philon d'Alexandrie*, ed. 2, Paris, 1925.

BRIERRE-NARBONNE, J. *Exégèse apocryphe des prophéties messianiques*, Paris, 1937.

BROWNLEE, W. H. "Biblical Interpretation among the Sectaries of the Dead Sea Scrolls", *Biblical Archaeologist* 14 (1951), 54–76.

BIBLIOGRAPHY

DAUBE, D. "Rabbinic Methods of Interpretation and Hellenistic Rhetoric", *Hebrew Union College Annual* 22 (1949), 239–64.

HEINEMANN, I. *Altjüdische Allegoristik*, Breslau, 1935.

—— "Die Allegoristik der hellenistischen Juden ausser Philon," *Mnemosyne* IV, 5 (1952), 130–8.

JOHNSON, A. R. "מָשָׁל", *Vetus Testamentum* Suppl. 3 (1955), 162–9.

MAASS, F. "Von der Ursprüngen der rabbinischen Schriftauslegung", *Zeitschrift für Theologie und Kirche* 52 (1955), 129–61.

MILIK, J. T. "Fragment d'un Midrash de Michée dans les manuscrits de Qumran", *Revue biblique* 59 (1952), 412–18.

RAPPAPORT, S. *Agada und Exegese bei Flavius Josephus*, Vienna, 1930.

ROWLEY, H. H. "The Nature of Prophecy in the Light of Recent Study", *Harvard Theological Review* 38 (1945), 1–38.

SHROYER, M. J. "Alexandrian Jewish Literalists", *Journal of Biblical Literature* 55 (1936), 261–84.

SIEGFRIED, C. *Philo von Alexandria als Ausleger des Alten Testaments*, Jena, 1875.

STEIN, E. *Die allegorische Exegese des Philo aus Alexandreia*, Giessen, 1929.

WOLFSON, H. A. *Philo* I–II, Cambridge, Mass., 1947.

3. THE LAW AND THE GOSPEL

BRANSCOMB, B. H. *Jesus and the Law of Moses*, New York, 1930.

COHEN, B. "Note on Letter and Spirit in the New Testament", *Harvard Theological Review* 47 (1954), 197–203.

DAVIES, W. D. *Paul and Rabbinic Judaism*, London, 1948.

GRANT, F. C. *Introduction to New Testament Thought*, New York, 1950.

HEMPEL, J. "Der synoptische Jesus und das Alte Testament", *Zeitschrift für die alttestamentliche Wissenschaft* 56 (1938), 1–34.

—— "On the Problem of the Law in the Old and New Testaments", *Anglican Theological Review* 34 (1952), 227–32.

KÜMMEL, W. G. "Jesus und der jüdische Traditionsgedanke", *Zeitschrift für die neutestamentliche Wissenschaft* 3 (1934), 105–30.

PRÜMM, K. "Israels Kehr zum Geist: 2 Kor 3, 17a im Verständnis der Erstleser", *Zeitschrift für katholische Theologie* 72 (1950), 385–442.

SCHOEPS, H. J. "Jésus et la loi juive", *Revue d'histoire et de philosophie religieuses* 33 (1953), 1–20.

SPICQ, C. *L'Épître aux Hébreux* I–II, Paris, 1952–3.

THACKERAY, H. St. J. *The Relation of St Paul to Contemporary Jewish Thought*, London, 1900.

WEISS, J. *Der erste Korintherbrief*, Göttingen, 1910.

WIKENHAUSER, A. "Die Traumgeschichte des Neuen Testaments in religionsgeschichtlicher Sicht", *Pisciculi F. Dölger*, Münster, 1939, 320–3.

WINDISCH, H. *Der zweite Korintherbrief*, Göttingen, 1924.

4. THE SECOND CENTURY

BARTH, C. *Die Interpretationen des Neuen Testaments in der valentinianischen Gnosis*, Texte und Untersuchungen 37, 3, Leipzig, 1911.

BURKITT, F. C. "The Exordium of Marcion's Antitheses", *Journal of Theological Studies* 30 (1928–9), 279–80.

GOODENOUGH, E. R. *The Theology of Justin Martyr*, Jena, 1923.

GRANT, R. M. "The Decalogue in Early Christianity", *Harvard Theological Review* 40 (1947), 1–17.

—— "The Place of the Old Testament in Early Christianity", *Interpretation* 5 (1951), 186–202.

—— "Tatian and the Bible", *Texte und Untersuchungen* 63, Berlin, 1957, 297–306.

HARNACK, A. v. *Marcion: das Evangelium vom fremden Gott*, ed. 2, Leipzig, 1924.

HEINISCH, P. *Der Einfluss Philos auf die ältesten christlichen Exegese,* Münster, 1908.

KNOX, J. *Marcion and the New Testament*, Chicago, 1942.

LABRIOLLE, P. de *La crise montaniste*, Paris, 1913.

MAURER, C. *Ignatius von Antiochien und das Johannesevangelium*, Zürich, 1949.

MOUSON, J. "Jean-Baptiste dans les fragments d'Héracléon", *Ephemerides Theologicae Lovanienses* 30 (1954), 301–22.

PREUSCHEN, E. *Die apokryphen gnostischen Adamschriften*, Giessen, 1900.

QUISPEL, G. *Ptolémée: Lettre à Flora*, Paris, 1949.

SAGNARD, F. M. *Clément d'Alexandrie: Extraits de Théodote*, Paris, 1948.

—— *La gnose valentinienne et le témoignage de saint Irénée*, Paris, 1947.

SCHOEPS, H. J. *Theologie und Geschichte des Judenchristentums*, Tübingen, 1949.

—— *Urgemeinde—Judenchristentum—Gnosis*, Tübingen, 1956.

WINDISCH, H. *Der Barnabasbrief*, Tübingen, 1920.

WOTTKE, F. "Papias", Pauly-Wissowa, *Realencyclopädie der classischen Altertumswissenschaft* XVIII 2 (1949), 966–76.

5. ALEXANDRIAN ALLEGORISTS

BARDY, G. "Les traditions juives dans l'œuvre d'Origène", *Revue biblique* 34 (1925), 217–52.

BIGG, C. *The Christian Platonists of Alexandria*, ed. 2, Oxford, 1913.

BIBLIOGRAPHY

BOER, W. DEN. *De Allegorese in het Werk van Clemens Alexandrinus*, Leiden, 1940.

BURGHARDT, W. J. "On Early Christian Exegesis", *Theological Studies* 11 (1950), 78–116.

CADIOU, R. *La jeunesse d'Origène*, Paris, 1935.

CAMELOT, T. *Foi et gnose*, Paris, 1945.

—— "Clément d'Alexandrie et l'écriture", *Revue biblique* 53 (1946), 242–8.

DANIÉLOU, J. *Origène*, Paris, 1948.

HANSON, R. P. C. *Origen's Doctrine of Tradition*, London, 1954.

KLOSTERMANN, E. "Ueberkommene Definitionen im Werke des Origenes", *Zeitschrift für die neutestamentliche Wissenschaft* 37 (1938), 54–61.

—— "Formen der exegetischen Arbeiten des Origenes", *Theologische Literaturzeitung* 72 (1947), 203–8.

LÄUCHLI, S. "The Polarity of the Gospels in the Exegesis of Origen", *Church History* 21 (1952), 215–24.

—— "Die Frage nach der Objektivität der Exegese des Origenes", *Theologische Zeitschrift* 10 (1954), 175–97.

LUBAC, H. DE. *Histoire et Esprit: l'intelligence de l'écriture d'après Origène*, Paris, 1950.

MOLLAND, E. *The Conception of the Gospel in the Alexandrian Theology*, Oslo, 1938.

MONDÉSERT, C. *Clément d'Alexandrie*, Paris, 1944.

PETERSON, E. "Zur Textkritik des Clemens Alexandrinus und Euagrios", *Theologische Literaturzeitung* 56 (1931), 69–70.

WOLFSON, H. A. *The Philosophy of the Church Fathers* I, Cambridge, Mass., 1956, 24–72.

INDEXES

1. BIBLICAL PASSAGES
Including Apocrypha and Pseudepigrapha

OLD TESTAMENT

NEW TESTAMENT

APOSTOLIC FATHERS

ANONYMOUS WRITINGS OR PSEUDEPIGRAPHA

2. BIBLICAL PASSAGES GIVEN EXEGESIS BY ANCIENT AUTHORS

OLD TESTAMENT

L*

NEW TESTAMENT

APOSTOLIC FATHER

3. ANCIENT AUTHORS

PAGAN

GNOSTIC AND/OR HERETICAL

4. MODERN AUTHORS